THINGS THAT MATTER

A Practical Guide for Leadership & Life

Lonnie Alcantara Essex

Monarch Hill LLC

Copyright © 2025 by Lonnie Alcantara Essex

All rights reserved.

No part of this publication may be reproduced, distributed, or transmitted in any form or by any means, including photocopying, recording, or other electronic or mechanical methods, without the prior written permission of the publisher, except in the case of brief quotations embodied in reviews and certain other non-commercial uses permitted by copyright law.

ISBN (paperback): 979-8-9998738-1-1

ISBN (eBook): 979-8-9998738-0-4

Monarch Hill LLC

Contents

Foreword 1
Introduction 3
Chapter 1: My Personal Journey to Leadership 9
    The Truth of Leadership 9
    Soddy-Daisy, Tennessee 10
    Command and Control 17
    18 Acres 23
    Things That Matter 26
    Summary 27
Chapter 2: TTM Framework and Core 29
    Framing Up TTM 29
    Core TTM 34
        Effective Communication 35
        Listening 37
        Ownership 38
    Summary 40
Chapter 3: Transformational and Aspirational TTM 43
    Transformational TTM 43
        Transparency 45
        Acknowledge Contributions 48
        Employee First 49
        Predictive Follow-Up 52
    Aspirational TTM 55
        Seek Assistance 55
        Continuous Improvement 58
        Curiosity 60
    Summary 62
Chapter 4: Discovering Our Things That Matter 65
    Creating a Template 66
    Netting It Out 67
    Step 1: Write First, Edit Later 69
    Step 2: Internal and External Validation 72

 Step 3: Maintain and Sustain 76
 Sources of Inspiration 78
 Summary 82
Chapter 5: Communicating Our Things That Matter 83
 The Root of it All 83
 Just Because You're Right, Doesn't Mean You Win 85
 Know Your Audience 88
 Being Present, Participating, and Playing Back 92
 Clarifying Questions 95
 Speak Your Truth 95
 Stand and Deliver 98
 Writing with Style 100
 Summary 101
Chapter 6: Demonstrating Things That Matter 103
 Interviewing for Things That Matter 105
 Have a Plan 109
 Get Action 111
 When a Mistake Becomes a Virtue 112
 One Foot on the Gas and One on the Brake 114
 Encoding Things That Matter 116
 Don't Outrun the Supply Wagon 119
 Summary 120
Chapter 7: Living Things That Matter 121
 Seven Levels of Done 129
 Influence vs. Control 132
  Control 133
  Influence 134
  Work Around (With Caution) 136
  Move On 137
 What Matters to You? 139
Epilogue: Coming Home 141
 Lonnie's Favorite Sayings 144
Acknowledgement 145

Foreword

In my very first meeting with Lonnie, I asked him: *What matters most to you? What kind of leader do you aspire to be? One who chases titles, or one who leaves a legacy?* We then launched into a deep discussion about the essence of leadership. Is it defined by accolades, titles, strategies? Or is it something deeper—the ability to inspire, uplift, and lead with purpose?

Over the past two decades, I've had the privilege of working alongside Lonnie Alcantara Essex. In that time, I've witnessed firsthand the essence of his leadership that transcends conventional metrics. I recall a pivotal moment during a challenging project for our federal government business. The stakes were high, and the pressure to avoid mistakes was immense. Yet, Lonnie remained steadfast—not in pursuit of personal glory, but in ensuring his team's success and well-being. It was a testament to his belief that leadership is about elevating everyone around you.

Within these pages, you won't find a theoretical roadmap, but rather lessons lived—stories forged from triumphs and setbacks alike. You'll discover insights that resonate with anyone who values purpose, excellence, and humanity.

This book delves into those very principles—the "things that matter" in leadership. It's not about the superficial trappings of success but about Lonnie's deep-rooted values that have guided his decisions and helped shape cultures and left a lasting impact.

This book is a map not of how to lead fast—but of how to lead well. It shows how purpose outlasts plans, how empathy outlives expediency, and how values outshine victories.

Lonnie has written a book that demonstrates a way of leading that will inspire readers to lead with heart and vision. So, take this as your invitation—and this book as your companion—into what's possible when leadership is rooted in things that matter.

George O'Meara
Former SVP Cisco Systems

Introduction

There comes a point in most people's careers when they look back and are surprised at just how much ground they've covered and at how varied the landscape has been. To move forward, sometimes you have to reflect on how far you have come. Looking back on my own career, I can see the many miles I have traveled on my leadership adventure. I can recall the hills I've climbed and the valleys I've rested in as well as the rough patches that slowed me down and the green fields that inspired me to carry on. It has been a long and satisfying journey, and I know I still have much further to travel. The best is yet to come!

Throughout my career, I have filled many roles, starting at the bottom in technology as a hands-on technical specialist and working my way up through various levels of leadership. I have been a program manager, program director, sales director, and general manager as well as others. Currently, I'm a vice president and general manager in a major corporation; I'm a co-owner and COO of a family-owned real estate investment firm; and I'm a coach and mentor to aspiring leaders and seasoned professionals. In these capacities and others, I'm often asked about leadership.

From professionals aspiring to become leaders, I often hear, "How do you become one?" Fair enough. A good direct question and a good place to start. From those who are already leaders, I'm usually asked, "How do you become a better one?" Also, a good question.

INTRODUCTION

The leadership journey, I tell you, is unique to each person who pursues it. Because of that, I can't give you a map. What I can give you, however, are lessons I have learned on my own journey. I can also offer a compass to help you toward your personal goals by first becoming grounded in your own principles and beliefs or, as I like to call them, Things That Matter. I wrote this book to help you discover your Things That Matter, a process which I believe will greatly aid you in your personal leadership quest.

The book starts by reflecting on my childhood experiences. It provides valuable insights into how we are challenged with overcoming adversity and even tragedies in our personal lives and how I was able to move past things that happen to all of us. I then cover the mistakes I made along the way and how I was able to learn from those mistakes and even grow. Lastly, I provide a framework for you to establish your own Things That Matter to give you a foundation for becoming a better leader and a better person in life.

Throughout our careers, we may be given titles such as manager, supervisor, director—monikers designating that one has oversight over multiple people or teams. More than likely, you'll have to earn those titles through outstanding performance. We all have to compete with others and differentiate ourselves from the crowd. Further, if you want to keep those titles and advance to others, you will have to maintain your track record and consistently deliver exceptional results. No one said it was going to be easy.

Those titles, however, don't automatically bestow upon us the attributes needed to be a leader. The fact is, you can be a manager but never ascend to becoming a leader. Conversely, you can be a leader without being a manager or even having a title at all. Many people confuse the role of manager with the role of leader. Managers, as the name suggests, manage things and are focused on *how* to do things. They tend to be operational. They manage resources, schedules, budgets, and projects. Leaders, on the other hand, are focused on *what* to do. Leaders take what needs to be accomplished and then inspire others to achieve common goals. You can be both, but being a manager doesn't by default make you a leader. This is a common misconception.

Another misperception is that leaders are limited to the workplace. The truth is, we can be leaders within our families, both immediate and extended. We can be leaders in our faith communities, not-for-profit organizations, local sports teams. Most organizations of any sort will have leaders, not just companies and businesses.

In addition, you can become a strong leader whether you're an introvert or extrovert. I often mentor professionals who fear they aren't outgoing enough to be leaders. Many are surprised that good leaders practice a fair amount of introspection. As we will see, you won't get very far in leadership without knowing yourself. In fact, leadership starts within each of us first. We need to lead first with ourselves and then with others.

The reality is that leadership has little to do with personality and everything to do with developing skills and impact. I'm typically viewed as an introvert, but I can become more of an extrovert or ambivert to meet the needs of any situation, meaning I can enjoy social interactions but also value my alone time. Situations, as you may have seen, often draw people into leadership roles. In a crisis, for instance, some individuals emerge as leaders even amongst strangers where no one is necessarily in charge. Although some may take on the mantle of leadership reluctantly, they rise to the occasion as if by a sense of duty or responsibility. In every natural or national disaster, we always find individuals stepping up to be leaders.

Whether you are a leader by design or by chance, whether you are new to a leadership role, a seasoned veteran, or aspiring to become a leader, this book can benefit you. Much of the material is focused on the early career leader, but it can also benefit entrepreneurs who are small business owners and experienced leaders who may need a fresh perspective. Most leadership journeys have unexpected twists and turns—the road to leadership is rarely swift or straight! Along the way, we may discover the need to re-invent ourselves at times. Don't be surprised and don't be disappointed if this happens to you. It happens to the best of us.

On our journeys, some will be with many employers while others may remain with the same company for their entire careers. You may find yourself stuck in a job or career field that you're unhappy with. My advice: find something that you love to do and that you're good at and do more of that, even if it means a whole new career path. It's never too late to find your place in life where you can do what you enjoy and have an impact! Of course, most of us need to earn a living to support our needs and our families, so be pragmatic.

I have had a long primary career in technology general management coupled with other side gigs such as residential real estate sales and real estate investment, coaching and mentoring, business and technology advisory services, and now writing. I love doing all these things and may do even more, and you can too.

As I have noted, along my leadership journey I have traveled many, many miles…both literally and figuratively. The things I learned from my experiences culminated in what I now call my Things That Matter (TTM). This book will explore each of my ten TTMs with examples of how and when I learned them. Moreover, the book will help you discover, communicate, demonstrate, and live your own Things That Matter. The beauty of TTM is that they are unique and specific to each of us. We all have things that matter to us, but few of us have taken the time to analyze, develop, and curate them into a defined set of principles and beliefs that can enhance how we live our lives. This book is not about learning my TTM, but rather it is a practical guide for you to develop your own.

I'm confident that reading and following the practices in this book will be a valuable experience for you. If taken with an open mind and a willingness to learn, it can give you a solid foundation on which to build your confidence and leadership skills. Leadership is not a destination but a journey. I believe TTM can be an important guide as you develop and sharpen your leadership skills. I wish you all the best on your adventure, and I am honored you have chosen this book to help you along your way.

As you progress through your TTM development, please contact me via my website at LonnieEssex.com should you have any questions or require any additional resources.

Chapter 1: My Personal Journey to Leadership

The Truth of Leadership

There are a lot of myths about leadership. The most prevalent one is that only a few select people are gifted with the ability to lead. That is, leadership is encoded in their DNA from birth. The myth suggests that people are either born to lead or destined to follow. Quite a grim outlook, if you ask me.

It's been my experience that leadership comprises a set of skills, attitudes, and behaviors that most people can develop over time. There are some foundational attributes that are needed, such as the willingness to learn and a desire to excel, but most people can become leaders. Again, leadership is not reserved just for a select few.

The sad truth is, however, that many people who *do* have the capacity to lead *don't* believe they can. They've either been told they don't have what it takes, or, and I think this is the case for many, they've convinced themselves that they aren't leadership material. Either way, it comes down to a lack of confidence. From my experience, confidence stems from knowing who you are on the inside. The leadership journey, in this respect, starts from within.

Most people think about leadership as a position or a role, which is why there is so much confusion between the concept of manager versus leader. A manager is a role; a leader is a person who inspires others to achieve common goals, who sees what needs to be done or sets the standard for what needs to be done along with a vision of the destination. The thought of becoming a leader first occurs to most people as they begin to plot out their career paths. Often, it's in response to the question: *Where do you see yourself in five years?* Here, someone might search through the company's org chart, looking at tier upon tier of titles and positions, wondering how high they could climb and how long it would take them.

Others may not think about leadership from a workplace context at all but from a more personal perspective as they seek to become a leader in their communities, their faith organizations, or even in their own homes or extended families. Again, leadership is not a role. Often, innovators have a great idea for a new product or service which could result in a new business venture. Almost daily we see innovation at work with new business startups around software apps and other gadgets that fill a need in our daily lives. Entrepreneurs quickly find that they had a great idea and maybe early success and then start to add other people in terms of employees and partners only to realize they need help with leadership to make it all work together in harmony and to keep the progress going and their new business venture viable.

I believe leadership is a worthy aspiration in whatever context one chooses to pursue it. I also believe that leadership is not a selfish aspiration. Leadership isn't about power, and it isn't about money. These are also myths. The truth is, the core purpose of leadership is to help others be their best and to achieve their goals. And in that spirit, I would like to invite you on a journey, a journey of discovering the sometimes-hidden leader inside of you.

Soddy-Daisy, Tennessee

My own path to leadership started at an early age, certainly not as any sort of prodigy—again, I don't subscribe to the theory that leadership is ingrained in one's genes—but rather as an observer and recipient of leadership (See some of my past influential leaders in the Acknowledgement section). And while that may sound stodgy and formal, trust me, it was anything but. My first experiences with leadership were within my family and my community.

I grew up in Soddy-Daisy, a small rural town in southeastern Tennessee (near Chattanooga). Today the population tops 13,000, but when I was a child, it was just chinning 4,000. No thriving metropolis by any means, but in the eyes of the youngest child of five with a WWII Marine Corps vet father and a loving, hardworking mother, it was my world.

By today's standards, and even the standards back then, my family was relatively poor. Certainly, there were others who had it harder than us, but also many who had it much better. In business, we might characterize it as bottom quartile. Regardless, I didn't realize we were poor the same way a fish doesn't know it's wet. It was just how life was, and I had nothing else to measure it by. What I did have, however, was my father's example. He was generous and benevolent, always helping others even when we appeared in need. As I think back on it now, I see that while we were poor in material things; we were wealthy in heart.

My father ran a small community grocery store. Allow me to clarify: we aren't talking about a massive 20,000-square-foot superstore selling everything from lawnmowers to sushi; we're talking about a 1,200-square-foot building made of white painted bricks and blocks. Up front, the floor was unpainted concrete, while at the back it was mostly hardwood. Old industrial shelves and appliances lined the walls and carved out aisles. The lumber for the framing was repurposed from an old home in the neighborhood. It was solid oak, and you could still see the marks of the circular saws used to size it. It felt like the whole building was held together with rusty nails, sweat, and sheer tenacity.

The store was also an Esso gas station. Not a lot of people remember Esso. Standard Oil of New Jersey used the brand from about 1926 to 1972. In later years, they switched to the more familiar Exxon. Today, there are still Esso stations in Europe and Canada. Every time I see one, I think of our store in Soddy-Daisy.

Back then, if you had told us that in fifty years most homes in America would be equipped with digital camera security systems, we would have thought a UFO had left you behind. At closing time, we'd lock the front door by placing a long screwdriver into the door frame to hold the door closed. No ADT or Ring. There was very little crime, and besides, there wasn't a lot to take.

As far as products, we sold vegetables, including some that we grew, and fish that we caught from our commercial fishing business, which was also a family operation. We also sold canned goods and other sundries, but it was very much a team effort. For instance, all the kids in the family worked in the store and in our commercial fishing business. We didn't have registers, only a cash drawer. Self-serve wasn't even a dream. To check customers out, we would take a paper grocery bag, write the prices in a neat column, sum it all up, add the tax from a little card, and then write out the total. The bag was the receipt. Everything served multiple purposes.

Sodas back then came in glass bottles. We had wooden crates to put the recyclable empties in at the front of the store. Patrons would come in and use them as stools, and people would gather round and chat, whether they needed groceries or not. The store was sort of a natural community center, and my father was someone people would just talk to. They'd share their problems and he, in turn, would share his advice or a helpful word. Over time, he became aware of people's situations throughout the town, and he wasn't the type of man who could stand around doing nothing while others suffered.

I have distinct memories of my sisters, my brother, and me delivering boxes and sacks of groceries to people all over town who were in need. We also helped people work on their houses and land. If there was a need, my dad was always willing to help. Where he could, he did it anonymously, but either way, he never accepted payment other than a simple "thank you."

I have to stress that throughout all this we had our own hardships. There's that expression about the cobbler's children having no shoes.

While we didn't go without shoes and we always had food to eat, we never rose very far above the poverty line.

During those years, my dad was always there for us. Much later, I would find out he was there for others as well in ways beyond charity and labor and helping hands. He mentored friends and family alike, teaching kids how to hunt, how to fish, how to fix and mend things. In those days, being self-sufficient could make the difference between surviving or not, so these were serious life skills. While I couldn't have put a name to it back then, what I was witnessing was leadership in action. What I absorbed from his example were values I still hold on to today, ideas I strive to live up to…or simply—Things That Matter.

While all this may seem idyllic, my father was also tough on us. He expected obedience and demanded discipline. But he also showed tough love, kindness, and fairness. He was our protector and a protector for others in need. I think I probably could have lived my entire childhood in that world and would have been happy, but life has its twists, often harsh and even cruel.

I'm sure at this point the reader is wondering about my mother. Where was she in all this?

My mother, Mary Catherine, died in a car accident when I was only four years old. Four of us kids were in the car with her at the time. My mother was benevolent and warm and "never met a stranger." Three of my siblings—my sisters—were severely injured. I was injured as well, but not nearly as badly. We had three hospital beds lined up in our home for months. This was in the late sixties. As much as people complain about our medical system today, healthcare back then was primitive in comparison, but we were thankful for it.

Many of the memories I have of working in the grocery store occurred during this time period. My siblings and I all ran the store independently. Even when I was nine years old, there were times I ran the store completely on my own, as did my siblings. All of us had to help carry the weight of becoming leaders without even knowing that was happening. The older kids worked other jobs, and all of us made our way through school. And it wasn't just stocking shelves and tendering sales; we did the books and ledgers for the store at the end of each day. There were so many lessons I learned back then. It instilled a sense of responsibility and ownership at a very deep level. Even now, some fifty years later, I apply those things I learned back then, both personally and professionally.

Through it all, my father was a tremendous force of good, to say the least. He led our family through an extremely difficult time. He had just lost his wife, who was thirty-eight at the time, and he had five children to raise. He embodied a steadfastness that's rarely seen today, and he never complained or blamed society or fell into self-pity.

It seemed like there was nothing but adversity all around, but we all got through it by the grace of God. Family and friends reciprocated the kindness my father had shown them over the years. It was a virtuous cycle. I believe that much of the wisdom my dad shared in those years was hard won through the difficulties he endured in the Great Depression and the war and in his personal life. Things like that can destroy people. For my father, they were a refiner's fire. In our grocery store, others from the community would gather around to swap stories and life lessons. My father was the center of the discussions and listened to everyone and dispensed advice to help others as needed.

He led by example, and those examples weren't lost on me. It just made sense in my young mind that good deeds and hard work naturally led to positive outcomes. After all, I learned from these examples through my father, our extended family, and our community. Today, I might reframe it as, "True leadership inspires a culture of reciprocity and goodwill."

Sadly, his example or today what we call true leadership, as good as it was, would prove to be short-lived. My father passed away from chronic liver disease when he was fifty. I was only twelve at the time. My siblings and I all lived together. My older sister, who was in her late twenties, became my legal guardian and head of the household. This was 1975. She ran the household, worked full time, made all the important decisions, financials, healthcare, everything. Like my father, she never complained. My other siblings, all older than me, pitched in as well to make our home life as good as it could be. Especially my two oldest sisters.

I have to believe that throughout her childhood she had learned the values she would need too during this challenging time from the examples she had grown up with. She learned them, absorbed them and emulated them in a way that was completely natural for her. She didn't spend nights reading books on leadership; she didn't watch Ted Talks; she didn't even have time to go to the gym or do yoga; she just did what she had to do—which was to lead and love and care for a household of five.

Right after my father passed away, my brother and I asked our sister, now our legal guardian, "What will we do now?"

My older sister replied, "We are going to stick together and get through this."

My family believed in the power of prayer, and we needed that to get through these hard times. A lesson that still applies today when we are faced with hardship and tragedy and that applies to all parts of life.

When I think about examples of leadership from my childhood, I think of my father. I think of the type of person you have to be to carry on under that type of adversity. I think of virtuous cycles of reciprocity that can come from those behaviors and ripple through an entire community. I also think of my sister, who instinctively picked up the mantle of leadership and gave so much of herself. And here's the thing: she probably never even thought about it that way. She just did what needed to be done.

Of course, she wasn't alone in all this. We all pitched in because this was a team effort. My two older sisters and extended family as well—aunts, uncles, cousins, and our church—were all there to help. Again, that virtuous cycle of benevolent leadership comes into play. If you grow up in a small town and you own a business that serves the community, everyone is very close. I had thirty-two first cousins, countless aunts, uncles—everyone made sure that we were okay. Needless to say, that doesn't take the hardship away, especially the emotional toll, but the importance of our support system cannot be understated.

We all grew up quickly, which is a natural byproduct of losing your parents at such a young age. Our family developed the ability to recover from adversity and grow from the challenge. I developed a need to stay productive—not needlessly busy, but productive. I had a full-time job; I went to school, and I had side jobs. It's a tendency that I maintain even now. Today I have a side real estate investment company, I coach and mentor people, I'm on a few boards, and I'm a genealogist for my family. Same tendency, different magnitude. I'm also the chef in the house and plan and cook virtually all our meals, which I enjoy. My father did the same.

I was a fairly bright and focused student. I advanced a full year and graduated when I was only sixteen. By then, I was working full time and running my side jobs, completely supporting myself. Instead of going to college, I leveraged my experience in our grocery store to land a job for a large grocery chain, where I very quickly became a manager.

I did that for a few years. As a young manager—I was seventeen when I began and nineteen when I left—I managed employees much older than me, had accountability for a two-million dollar per annum P&L, and was responsible for total client satisfaction for my department, the largest in the company.

I had come a long way since the days of our family's grocery store in Soddy-Daisy. I had learned some hard lessons, some that I cherished, some that I would rather not have faced. But that's the thing about life—adversity plays a role in everyone's life. And while we may have no choice about how or when difficulties may arise, I firmly believe we decide whether those hardships will destroy us or temper us. We all must learn from our mistakes and learn how to move forward in the face of adversity in life. I do that by staying productive and by giving back, while teaching others to give back. My Things That Matter keep me grounded and enable me to help others. Later in this book, you will have an opportunity to develop your own Things That Matter.

By the age of nineteen, I had already achieved some degree of success, but I had a strong desire to learn more and do more. I wanted to see the world, not just on a television or movie screen, but in person. So, I did what a lot of young men in the US choose to do at this juncture in their lives—I joined the military.

Command and Control

In the military, I was exposed to a very different leadership than I had seen with my father or even in the grocery world. For one, it was more disciplined and controlled. The military is nothing if not systematic. There is also a strict chain of command, a hierarchy that has to be followed at all times. As a leadership style, it is commonly called Command and Control. These attributes are fairly easy to see from the outside. The uniforms, the ranks, the saluting, the 'Yes, sir, no, sir."

What is not so easy to see from the outside is that the military teaches service members a lot about taking care of others, listening and not just hearing, learning from mistakes, and taking ownership. I'm sure I didn't see these words in the recruitment material I was provided when I joined, but they became self-evident as I progressed through the ranks.

A large portion of personal and professional growth in the military comes from a wide variety of training and development programs. While the US military is well known for its extensive formal training, there are also coaching, mentoring, and even sponsorship activities. All of these programs are vital, but the majority of growth, the lessons that really sink in and become part of who you are, occur through hands-on experiences of regular everyday military life both on and off the job. In short, in the military, one is immersed in an environment built to ensure development. Not everyone takes full advantage of this, and it is sometimes hard to recognize amongst the drills and regimentation, but it is there for those who want it and seek it out.

At nineteen and newly enlisted in the US Air Force, this immense world of possibility was opened for me, and I was determined to make the most of it. I spent six months full-time in Air Force Technical

Training. I had scored the minimum aptitude level for acceptance into a technical career field. This had two major impacts on me. For one, I was humbled. I had always done exceptionally well in academics, and here I barely chinned the bar to get into the training I wanted. Clearly, I was in a different world, a world of exceptionally high standards, a world that did not accept excuses for underperformance. Second, I was determined to excel regardless of how hard I had to work for it. Ironically, that low entry score inspired me to work harder than I would have if I had aced the exam. So, I applied myself like never before. A hundred and eighty days later, I graduated with honors at the very top of my class.

Following technical training, my first assignment was at Andrews Air Force Base (now Joint Base Andrews) in Maryland. It felt like a new beginning, which it was. At the time, it was the farthest away from home I had ever been. Of course, that would soon change. I wanted to see the world, and the Air Force was happy to oblige.

While stationed at Andrews, I was assigned to a large communications group. Communications here referred to the technical variety as opposed to public or media relations. The experience opened my eyes to the innovative ways technology could be applied. I learned how to solve problems and became an expert in troubleshooting. My job as a technical controller was to be an expert across all types of systems and to be able to isolate faults and remediate them quickly to provide mission-critical communications to military commanders. This still applies to business and life today as it relates to pragmatic, step-by-step problem solving. I learned quite a bit about practical applications of the field, but, more valuable, I learned about leadership from the senior individuals who mentored me.

You have to be willing to learn if you want to lead. More than that, you have to be coachable. There is a difference. Most people can readily learn, but it takes both humility and respect to make yourself vulnerable and to be coachable. Books and online tutorials can only take you so far. I firmly believe it takes actual human interaction to truly grow and develop by drawing on the knowledge and experiences of others. Thankfully, my assignment in the Communications Group afforded me many opportunities to be taught as we worked together on assigned teams, learning from each other.

My next assignment was based in the Azores, an autonomous region of Portugal in the middle of the Atlantic Ocean—the end of the world, literally. When I was told where I was going, I had to look it up on a map. A very large, detailed map. I was assigned to a Portuguese air base at Lajes Field on the island of Terceira.

I was bright, energetic, and eager to learn—everything the military wanted from a young recruit back then. In the movies, they call this being "gung ho." Keeping in mind where I came from, I was driven to achieve. There is something about growing up in hardship and near poverty that pushes one forward. It's a hard motivator, certainly, but it has its benefits. For one, most people who grow up under such conditions have a keen desire never to go back to that standard of living. It creates drive. Second, having to face and overcome obstacles at an early age over a sustained period of time builds a type of muscle memory. Such muscle memory is hard-earned, but it can and will prove to be a healthy habit later in life and lead to grit and intestinal fortitude.

In the military, practices like doing your job to the best of your ability, following command, and making clear, rational decisions based on data and facts while under strict timelines or other pressures…well, all that seemed straightforward to me. Not always easy, but straightforward. I excelled in that environment. As a result, I was promoted early, quickly, and often through the enlisted ranks and into early supervisory and management roles. And while that may sound easy as I summarize it here, it wasn't such a cakewalk when I lived it in day-to-day reality back then.

The military is obviously based on a rank system and is very hierarchical. There's a chain of command, and you follow it. It's an effective system that delivers results. In fact, crisis response teams for industries all over the world follow a similar principle with unified command centers that are instituted in the face of major incidents or emergencies. It has its positives and negatives. On the upside, it creates a high degree of order; on the downside, it limits people to what they can do based on their rank. If you're going to be in the military, that's just the way it is.

For me, I had to overcome the fact that I was young, in the early stages of my career, and held a relatively low rank. As such, I had to make the most of every opportunity I was given because there weren't a lot of them. They were scarce and couldn't be wasted. My strategy was simple: work hard and apply what expertise I had in the hopes that opportunities would yield themselves. What I had in my favor was my academic learning, technical training, strong work ethic, and good life values. I also had a fair amount of intestinal fortitude, which is a polite way of saying I could put up with a lot without getting fazed. I saw plenty of people in the military who fell victim to their short tempers or an inability to cope with stress. In this regard, my early years had prepared me well.

To enact this coping strategy, one of the tactics I took was to push to earn placement on special assignments where I could demonstrate more impact. At the time, the US government had flying command posts all over the world to respond at a global level to national emergencies. The European Airborne Command post was moving to my location in the Azores, and I was assigned to coordinate key aspects of the mission, including overseeing the setup of the equipment, embedding the right protocols, and establishing processes to keep everything running smoothly. Again, I was still a relatively low-ranking, junior enlisted personnel, but the commander that I worked for, Lieutenant Colonel Alfred R. Garcia, Jr., saw I had the capacity to attend to all the details and the drive to inexhaustibly get it done. He entrusted me with a lot, and I worked hard to live up to that standard.

From a technological standpoint, it was my job to make sure the flying command post could execute commands via various communications systems, and, if all else failed, they were set up and able to authorize the launch of strategic weapons. Essentially, they were the last line of defense. Needless to say, the pressure was immense. The level of risk and the visibility were everything. And I did it. Not only did I do it, but I did it well.

One of the great things about the military is that you are measured on your impact and your effort. For all of my effort and impact, I was nominated as Airman of the Year for the US Forces, Azores, which was, at that time, under the command of the US Air Force. They picked twelve people in total from a candidate pool of hundreds of thousands to be awarded airmen of the year. My commander nominated me, and I was honored to have earned the distinction.

After that achievement, my commander asked me, "Essex," he always called me Essex, "how can I help you? What can I do for you?"

This was something I had pondered over many times ("What would I like to do next?"). The idea of challenging myself in an untried space has always been energizing for me. Call it curiosity, call it an industrious spirit, but being in a role that is going to test me and requires my full attention—that's something to get up in the morning for. I often thought about an assignment or location that would push me to stretch my skills, that would really require me to exercise new ways of thinking—an environment where real impact could be made. To me, there was nowhere else I could think of, at least in the United States, that matched this description more than the White House.

What the heck? I thought. *He asked an honest question; I'll give him an honest answer.*

"Well," I said, "sir, I would like to work at the White House."

He thought on it for a second or two, then said, "I have a friend there. Let me make a call. I'll get you in for an interview, and I'll write you a letter of recommendation." It was as simple as that. He asked a question, and I answered honestly. Of course, the long story was far from simple and included months of hard work, sleepless nights, and unbending resolve. I had to earn keep, if you will.

For his part, he made true on his promise. He opened that door for me. He didn't walk me through it and pave the way onward, but he did open it, and I will always be thankful to him for that. I went through an exhaustive series of panel interviews, background checks, and assessments. I wasn't the only candidate for the job, so there was competition as well. In the end, I was offered a role at the White House in the White House Communications Agency (WHCA), a prestigious joint military assignment that has been around for over eighty years.

Through that experience, I learned a valuable lesson about career progression and, more importantly, about myself. Sometimes the reward for doing a good job is earning additional money. A lot of people are driven by monetary compensation, and while I see the value of a good salary, I have to say money isn't my primary driver. Sometimes the reward for a job well done is a promotion or advancement. Again, career advancement was important for me during a certain stage in my career, but having a new title or grade code has never been a chief motivator for me.

And sometimes the reward is unlocking new opportunities. The principle became clear to me, and I would see it repeated again and again in my own career and that of others: a job well done can unlock opportunities. If you're ready, willing, and able, you can then make the most of those opportunities which, following more hard work, can lead to other opportunities. Similar to good leadership, performing well and striving to excel can be a virtuous cycle.

There will be setbacks. There always are. There will be plenty of times when hard work only leads to more hard work and sometimes even disappointment. Nothing in this world is guaranteed. Hard work can go unrecognized. You can't always expect to be rewarded for doing something well. As the saying goes, a job well done is its own reward. If you can't internalize that principle, then the going will indeed be tough. Tougher, in fact, than it has to be. The silver lining is that making mistakes or even taking a step backward can yield positive results, though at the moment it might be hard to see that mistakes are key to learning.

A mindset of perseverance, of intestinal fortitude, is needed to maintain forward momentum and to recover from faltering. One has to be persistent and consistent in the desire to achieve success and overcome adversity. Simply put, don't give up. Stick with the task at hand even when it gets tough…and it will. Setbacks become opportunities to learn and grow. Everyone has them, so don't be surprised when they happen to you.

18 Acres

My leadership lessons continued throughout my years working at the White House. I was in my early twenties in a position of high trust and high responsibility. It wasn't a political job; rather, it was a national security level job, which required very high clearances. I saw the president regularly, not occasionally, but regularly.

They say when you climb Mount Everest you have to be careful to pack in oxygen so you can breathe when you get up to the high reaches. The air gets thin, and even the smallest mistakes can cause catastrophic problems. Working in the White House felt like that. The stakes were high. You had to be entirely present 100% of the time—mentally alert, physically prepared. Every day was both exhausting and energizing.

My early experiences in the military helped prepare me for the role, as did my upbringing. I'll always be thankful for those who helped shape and guide me during those years. The lessons they taught me through their examples, words, and behaviors made all the difference. They were my oxygen as I climbed so many new heights. Who will provide your oxygen as you climb new heights?

My job as a senior networking specialist and program manager was to ensure that the president could carry out his role as commander-in-chief. This was squarely during the Cold War. I acted as a technology lead on presidential trips. In the White House, or the "18 Acres" as we called it, I was usually a shift supervisor working on a team of a few dozen specially trained individuals from all branches of the Armed Forces.

Our focus was technology, no-fail mission-critical communications, command and control, information security, logistics, transportation, program management, and other specialized disciplines. No-Fail in this situation meant the leader of the free world had to be available and accessible for any world crisis to consult with advisors, analyze inputs, make decisions and act instantly in a manner that would prevent catastrophic global events. There was simply no room for error. Therefore, a successful mission was the only option!

Mostly we worked behind the scenes in wherever the president and senior staff would go—every room, vehicle, and motorcade. To blend in, we only wore civilian clothes. It was only during special occasions and awards ceremonies away from the 18 Acres that we reverted to our military uniforms. We worked around the clock, covering every waking hour of the president, and traveled extensively to support him and other national security leaders anywhere in the world at any moment in time. Wherever we were needed, that's where we were.

As odd as it may seem, the habit I had developed in my youth of staying overly productive was still in high gear. Because of my relatively low military pay, I also had a side gig in commercial construction as a foreman for over two years while serving at the White House. Because I worked rotating shifts this allowed for regular periods of time off which provided availability for a side gig. In addition to the much-needed income boost, it allowed me to gain additional knowledge and skills in a separate field and get exposure to an entirely different environment than the regimented, high-stakes military setting I was used to.

In my role as senior networking specialist and program manager, I spent a lot of time in the White House itself, but I also spent several months working at President Reagan's Ranch, Rancho del Cielo, in Santa Barbara, California. I often saw and heard things that only the president and a few others were allowed. On occasion, I was asked by the designated military aide to temporarily secure the "Nuclear Football." This odd term refers to the briefcase that contains the plans and the codes required to launch a nuclear attack. This wasn't my regular responsibility, but the military aide, who was solely dedicated to this role, would occasionally hand me or someone from my organization the "football" for safekeeping. That in itself was a special kind of pressure.

The responsibilities were always high, and so were the consequences. Earned trust was a major factor here, and there were always methods to indicate who was to be trusted. In addition to a top-secret Department of Defense clearance and many special access programs, I was given a clearance known as "Yankee White" or YW. YW allowed close personal access to the president, the vice president, and senior staff as well as to extremely sensitive situations and information. If you were inside the 'circle of trust,' you were *inside*. Mistakes, errors, or breaches of any kind could quickly lead to being *outside* the circle. If you were outside, you simply could not do your job, and your career would come to a disappointing end. Maintaining confidentiality and reliability at all costs was paramount.

During this time, I also led or co-led multiple technology projects underneath the White House—that is, literally underneath the White House in what is often referred to as the "bunker." I worked with Cabinet level agencies, all the military branches, and other departments and agencies to support the mission, which was always no-fail. The work provided me with a unique perspective, especially in times of adversity and crisis.

Someone once asked me, "How do you remain calm in a crisis?"

"Well," I said, "it gets easier with experience." Sadly, the only way to learn to stay calm in a crisis is to go through more than one of them.

I can't say much more about this very special and highly impactful assignment other than that I remained open to learning and being taught and, as a result, I grew in ways that prepared me for greater things ahead.

I'm grateful for my experience at the White House and all the things that I had to do to ensure that we didn't fail. It was stressful, but I learned how to stay calm and remain level-headed when others may have panicked. Some might view those experiences as a burden; I view them as a responsibility I was asked to carry, a duty I was proud to fulfill. For my service, I received the Presidential Service Badge (#9120) as well as the Joint Service Commendation Medal. I have them framed, and they hang in my office.

Today, I'm still an active member of the 1600 Communications Association. The 1600 Communications Association is for current and former military members who serve in White House roles. Membership is for life. Similar to many high-stakes teams that work closely together, the bonds that are formed under that type of pressure last forever.

My story didn't end in the White House. From there, I embarked on a career in the private sector that has been as thrilling as it has been rewarding. As I think back, though, the kernels of my understanding of leadership were formed in my childhood and my early career in the military and at the White House. These principles would grow and evolve as I faced a wide range of challenges across a wide range of roles throughout my career, but they had their origin in those formative years.

Things That Matter

I began this chapter by noting that leadership is not an innate trait; that while it may seem that some people are born to leadership, the truth is that many can learn to lead. I also noted that there were some foundational needs that are prerequisites to begin the leadership journey. As harsh as it may sound, without these basic leadership traits, one need not apply. The good news is that those traits are accessible to most who want them. The Basic Leadership Traits:

1. The willingness to learn and to be taught
2. The drive to excel
3. The intestinal fortitude to push through challenges
4. The desire to help others.

Upon careful examination, one will see that three of these basic leadership traits are internally focused and one is externally focused. In truth though, the first three work in service of the fourth. <u>I believe that the desire to help others is the primary mission of leadership</u>.

I also believe leadership is not one-size-fits-all. Leadership shows up differently in each person. This is because each of us has our own values, which develop through our own unique experiences. I call these Things That Matter. Everyone has Things That Matter but few can readily identify or name them because few have taken the steps required to really focus on their own uniqueness in a structured framework. This is a problem. It is also an opportunity.

I believe every leader should be cognizant of the Things That Matter to them. Moreso, I believe every leader should be able to name and define the Things That Matter to them.

I also believe leaders should communicate their Things That Matter to the people they lead. Simply put: if these things matter to you, if they define how you lead, then you shouldn't keep them a secret. Things That Matter are meant to be shared.

And finally, I believe leaders should demonstrate their Things That Matter through their daily behaviors. If they are good, positive Things That Matter, then they will lead to good results and positive impacts…but they first have to be put into action.

Summary

In this chapter, I have shared my upbringing and the trajectory of my early career. I didn't do this out of vanity. I did it because within those experiences are the seeds that would grow into my Things That Matter. I expect any reader of this chapter could probably list several of my Things That Matter already, but I won't keep them a mystery. In the next several chapters, I'll discuss them in depth and provide stories and examples of how or why they came to matter to me.

My goal with this book is to help you discover your own Things That Matter so that you can use them in your leadership journey or your personal life, or both. In many ways, these two paths are tightly intertwined. During this process of helping you develop your Things That Matter, I will share with you my own Things That Matter. I call them TTM for short. There are ten, and I divide them into three categories: Core, Transformational, and Aspirational. I believe my

Core TTM can apply to most, if not all, leaders. My Transformational TTMs serve as inflection points for me. These have helped me to gain traction and to differentiate my leadership style. I can see where they could be helpful for others, but I also see Transformational TTM as a flex space. Aspirational TTM are all bespoke, and I would expect these to be different for every leader.

Leadership is a journey. Discovering your TTM is part of that journey. When I started on my own particular path in my hometown in Tennessee, I had no idea where it would lead me. In fact, it wasn't until mid-career before I even realized I was on a journey. Until then, I was just pushing to get ahead, to do better, to excel. If I only had a map, some direction…but, of course, I did. I had coaches, mentors, friends, and family who all showed me different aspects of leadership.

I am pleased to be with you on your journey. I hope Things That Matter can serve as a compass to understanding yourself, to developing your own unique leadership style, to building your confidence, and to helping you help others.

"As a young professional myself, this book resonated on a personal level. Like many aspiring leaders, I sometimes feel the pressure to prove myself quickly or to model my approach after others. Essex's message was a timely reminder that real leadership is about being grounded in my own values, showing up authentically, and focusing on helping others succeed. It gave me both clarity and reassurance that leadership is a path I can actively build, one step at a time."

Arthur Scudeler Brunetti, Retention Manager, Gozney

Chapter 2: TTM Framework and Core

Framing Up TTM

I vividly recall taking a leadership role at a company I had newly joined. I was inheriting a team of highly qualified professionals who knew nothing about me. My onboarding included multiple briefings and handover sessions. I received strategy documents, business plans, project charters, employee files—literally hours upon hours of meetings and volumes upon volumes of documentation which described my new organization, its functions, and all of its people.

On the other hand, my team, from direct reports down to entry-level employees, knew nothing about me except what they might have gleaned from my LinkedIn page or the announcement the company sent introducing me. I wondered how I could let them know my priorities and my expectations—and not just business priorities, but my own personal priorities, the Things That Mattered to me as a leader and as a person. How would they know what to expect from me? Sure, they might figure them out over the next several years, but who has that kind of time when you are on a thirteen-week delivery schedule, and having to produce positive results every quarter? I needed them to understand where I was coming from so that we could get to where we were going…together as a team.

I remember stepping onto the stage for my first town hall with the company. It wasn't my first public speaking event, of course. By that time in my career, I had presented to very small and very large groups of employees. This isn't to say I wasn't nervous. I was. The moment you stop being nervous about presenting is probably the day you need to quit, because it's a very good indication that you've stopped caring.

I had my prepared notes. I had slides to back me up, but I realized that what I wanted to say and what they needed to hear wasn't in the presentation deck. It was in my head, and it wasn't going to do anyone any good until I got it out and shared it. After a few introductory words, I simply said, "I want you to know what matters to me. I want you to know what to expect from me, and I want you to know what I expect from you." I then walked them through a short list of what I now call my Things That Matter. At that time, I had six, maybe seven. Over the years I would add several more, and even replace a few, until I arrived at the current round number of ten.

When the town hall was complete, I received excellent feedback. My staff saw me as accessible, and they felt they knew how to approach me. But it wasn't over then. Over the next several months, they watched for evidence that I really believed and lived my Things That Matter. For my part, I knew that once I spoke those words aloud, I had to consistently demonstrate them, or I would lose all my credibility and have zero chance of earning my team's trust. The short version of the story is that what I said aligned with how I behaved, and how I behaved helped lead our team to success. That's the power of knowing what things matter to you, communicating them effectively, and then "walking the talk."

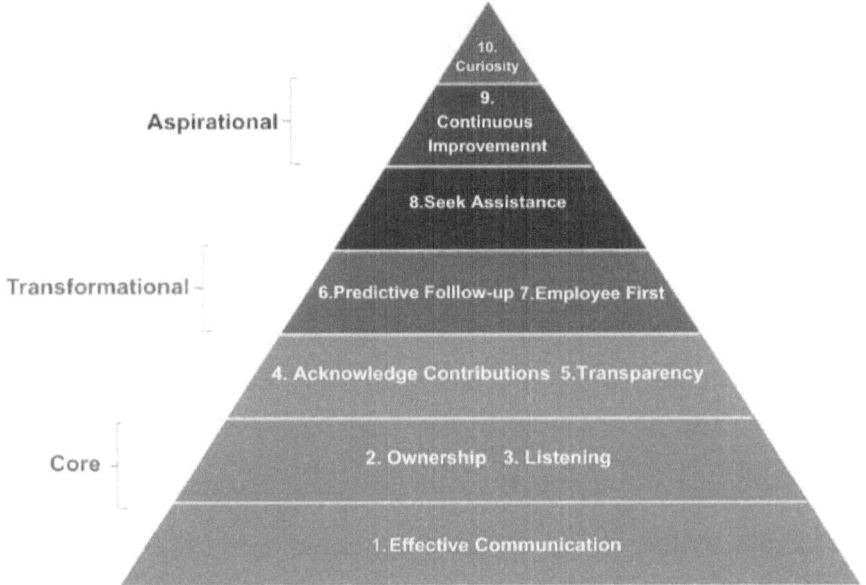

TTM Framework Pyramid

My first three Things That Matter have never changed. They were there on that day I walked out on the stage, and they are there today. In order, they are Effective Communication, Listening, and Ownership. If we use a pyramid model, they make up the bottommost layers, forming the foundation layers. I call them Core TTM. Without them, the pyramid topples. They are essential to my framework. In fact, they are so essential that I believe they should make the foundation of anyone's Things That Matter. I would be hard-pressed to think of a situation in which these three principles do not play a critical role in achieving your success. Whether in business, at home, or in the community, Effective Communication, Listening and Ownership are vital.

Topping the initial Core principles are four Transformational principles. They create a distinctive inflection point, which distinguishes my leadership approach from that of many others. I believe they are important factors in any leadership approach, but I can understand where they may differ for others depending on the industry or context.

In order, they are Transparency, Acknowledge Contributions, Employee First, and Predictive Follow-up.

The final three principles are Aspirational TTM. These I would absolutely expect to differ from leader to leader, reflecting the individual's unique style of leadership values. As the title "Aspirational" also suggests, these can be "stretch" principles. That is TTM that one is always striving to fully achieve but perhaps not quite getting there. My Aspirational TTM are Seek Assistance, Continuous Improvement, and Curiosity. Not only are these three TTM fairly distinctive to my personal leadership style, but they are ones I discovered later in my leadership journey. Effective Communication, for instance, was evident to me from my early, early career. In fact, I understood the value of Effective Communication before I even started my career. My penchant for Curiosity, however, developed much later in my career. It may have been there from the beginning, but it took longer for me to recognize how much it mattered to me and how large a role it actually played in my life.

Since that town hall meeting when I first shared my emerging list of Things That Matter, I've discussed them with employees, mentees, colleagues, family, and even friends. I've also had the chance to ask others what their Things That Matter might be. I find that most people, especially managers, have never given it any thought. Not that they don't have priorities or values or principles, but rather they simply have never thought of writing them out or formalizing them. I've always wondered, "Well, if you're not sure what they are and if you haven't documented and then shared them, where does that leave the people that you lead?"

I am a great lover of history. I especially like to study renowned leaders and communicators. My short list of favorites includes President Teddy Roosevelt, Prime Minister Winston Churchill, Rev. Martin Luther King, President Barack Obama, Prime Minister Margaret Thatcher, and President Ronald Reagan. They were all excellent communicators and were able to drive change, enrolling others to willingly and enthusiastically join their causes. Of these, President Roosevelt is one of my all-time favorites.

Teddy Roosevelt, who was born into prosperity, would often jump into a situation to learn more and help solve problems or make things better even though in most cases he really didn't have to. He took ownership when a void existed and then, once the problem was solved, he moved on to the next situation. President Roosevelt took steps to start the US National Park System that we all enjoy today. He also led efforts to deliver the Panama Canal to an entire world after many years of strife and uncertainty. You could say that when he faced a problem, he 'owned it.'

Ownership or taking responsibility is one of my Core TTM. I see it in Teddy Roosevelt's life story. I also see it in my father's life story. I have seen it many times in the military, and I see it every day in the business world. I have been privileged to work with successful leaders in so many areas of my career and life. On the one hand, you might say I adopted the principle of ownership from Teddy Roosevelt; on the other hand, I experienced it over and over again in my personal life and came to value it on my own terms. Ownership isn't a concept I created, or that is unique to me, but I have seen it play out in so many examples around me, and I consistently find that when I practice that value, things come out for the better. It just feels right.

In the spirit of ownership, I share with you my Things That Matter. Some may resonate with you; some may not. Some may reflect what you already believe; some may be totally foreign. However they resonate, I encourage you to think about each of them. Consider their merits; consider how they might play a role in your leadership journey. Doing so will help you to discover and identify your own Things That Matter.

Core TTM

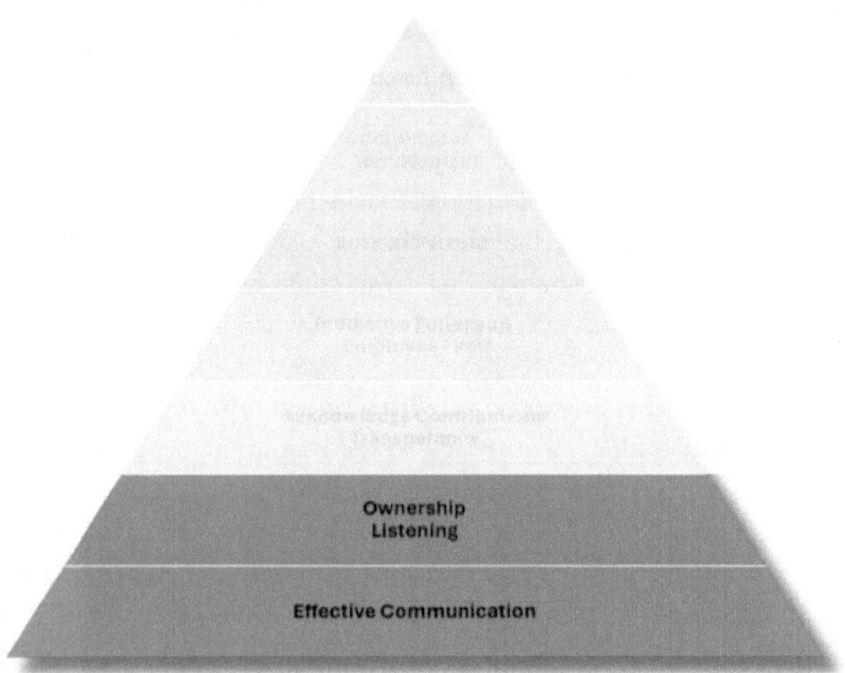

As I noted earlier, I arrived at my Core TTM early in my leadership journey, and I believe they should be foundational to anyone's TTM. Some may suggest my thinking is biased and largely shaped by the generation I grew up in. I admit that may be a factor. I also admit that my point of view may be Western-centric. We, after all, are all a product of our environment. But I also recognize that without these three values—Effective Communication, Listening, and Ownership—any leader will find it difficult to mobilize their teams or consistently deliver any kind of positive result. I am therefore constantly dismayed to see that these three fundamental qualities are missing in the basic skill sets of so many leaders today. For me, it is an easy fix. Simply do your best to adopt these principles, and I promise you they will make a notable difference in your ability to lead.

Effective Communication

My first Thing that Matters, the base of the TTM Framework Pyramid, is Effective Communication as clear and concise communication is often the cornerstone of success in any endeavor. Poor communication, that is not clear and concise, is the most prevalent problem in everything from customer service to interpersonal relationships to complex projects. If you want to excel in any of these areas and many more, you need to use clear and concise communication.

I first learned the value of Effective Communication when I was in middle school. For some reason, I thought it would be fun to run for class president. Not only did it seem like fun, but it seemed like a worthwhile endeavor, something that would have an impact.

As I walked around my school, I saw my opponents' posters hanging everywhere. They were the regular sort: smiling photo, name, and an uninspiring slogan which simply instructed the readers to vote for whoever was pictured on the poster. I shouldn't be too harsh in my judgement. This was middle school after all, and 'vote for me' was direct and clear. But I wanted something different. I wanted something the other students—my constituents—would remember me by, something that stood out from the crowd.

I had a friend named Harley at the time. In fact, he remains a friend to this day. Harley was an artist, and he was good, with a quirky and creative style. I asked him to create a catchy image of me—a caricature-like picture. We were in middle school, so cartoons and animation caught our attention. Harley was able to capture my essence, meaning you could tell it was me at a glance, but at the same time it was fun and exciting. Keep in mind this was the 1970s. Back then, most people had black and white televisions, and there were only three networks. There was no internet, no apps, no mobile phones. People listened to music on transistor radios. With that said, a caricature drawing done up in full color was out of the ordinary and attention-grabbing. That was strategy number one: be memorable.

My second strategy was a little tougher. I had to speak at election events, and I had to have something to say. Again, I was in middle school, so these weren't big town halls or anything major. Regardless of the size of the audience, the challenge was the same. In just a few minutes, I had to convey why my classmates should vote for me. I had to make it memorable, and I had to make actual sense. This is hard enough to do even as an adult. I was about thirteen years old!

At thirteen, I was too young to know the subterfuge in politics. So, I did the obvious thing, and I hoped it would work. I knew my audience. I grew up with them. I knew the things they were interested in. I knew what they expected of a class president. I also knew that I had to be authentic as I couldn't fool them with some crazy promises or long-winded messaging that no one would understand. We were kids. We got bored easily, and we liked things to be plain and simple. Complexity was for adults. And finally, they knew me. I grew up with these kids. They were my friends and neighbors for years. This meant I couldn't go up there and act like someone I wasn't. My approach, then, was to speak to their interests, keep it simple, and be myself. The end result was I not only won the election that year but also the year after.

Today when I talk to colleagues in communications, they tell me that Effective Communication involves knowing your audience, being clear and concise, and being authentic. Some things really never do change.

It has been a long time since middle school. Throughout my career, I have learned that communication crosses personal and professional boundaries and can determine the success or failure of any and all relationships. As a leader, if you want your ideas to be heard and to be accepted as genuine, you must master the skill of Effective Communication. It's amazing to me that the simple principles I used in middle school have played out throughout my career and in the world around me.

For example, when I worked in the White House, I saw firsthand how a single individual could effectively communicate to get other world leaders to join in and drive an end to communism in the old Soviet Union (USSR) and to essentially end the Cold War which had lasted for many decades. More recently, I have seen the consequences of ineffective communication at the same level, which have created dissension and division such as politics on the national and global stage where politicians cause more issues than they solve, while creating divisions. Consider social media fueled by an existing mis-trust from the citizens and you have ineffective communication.

Listening

The principle of Listening is closely related to Effective Communication. In fact, many say you can't have one without the other. Listening involves fostering an ethos of understanding, not merely waiting to reply. Listening comes in many forms: hearing the words, interpreting the messaging, watching body language, and even listening for what is not spoken. Listening involves being present, dedicating one's focus and energy to the person or matter at hand. How many times have we been in a work meeting, video call, or even at a social or family function where we are trying to have a meaningful conversation, but the other person is distracted by their phone or another person?

We trick ourselves into thinking we can multi-task. Science has shown that the human brain has evolved to process one thing at a time—there is no multitasking, there is only fast switching. While some people can weave a lot of thoughts and actions in rapid succession, most of us aren't able to fully listen to or comprehend multiple things at once without losing something significant in translation. In short, we have to be present in the moment to listen properly.

Whether at home or at the office, leaders especially need to take the time to listen, ask questions, and play back what they heard to fully understand the details and the situation. Otherwise, they may fail to get all the information. This failure can lead to bad decisions and poor choices. Good decisions come from listening, having good data, and having a complete view of a situation. A leader must make an investment in time to listen closely or risk paying for it later.

It's important to note that listening doesn't always pertain to literal hearing, as in discussions or conversations. Sometimes listening refers to more contextual situations as there are always three sides to every story. For instance, I recall an experience in which an employee in my organization was caught abusing company travel resources and assets. Let's call him Robert. Robert had a reputation as a good employee with a solid performance record. He was known to follow policy and protocol without fail. It was therefore a surprise to his management to find he had used company travel resources and money for personal travel.

My reaction as a young leader would have been to fire him on the spot and ask questions later which of course would be a mistake. He clearly violated policy; consequences must be paid. My reaction in this situation as a more experienced leader, however, was to ask Robert's direct manager to find out if he was okay. I encouraged the manager to not jump to conclusions.

"Talk to him first to see if he and his family are okay," I said. "Get the facts. All the facts. Find out if anything is happening in his life that might have led to this."

As requested, his manager gathered the facts and details. He discovered Robert had a personal family situation that he was struggling with and was making bad choices about using company resources. We worked out an appropriate solution, holding Robert responsible for his actions but also not ending his career or setting him back over the matter.

Now, I am not suggesting that leaders need to become deeply involved in all their employees' personal lives to ensure they have the optimal situations to thrive in the workplace. What I *am* saying is that leaders should make it a habit to move beyond their assumptions by listening. Listen to your customers, listen to your employees, listen to your family—try to understand what is truly happening in any given situation.

Ownership

The principle of Ownership is as simple as it is important. Embrace responsibility for your actions until completion, or until the responsibility is duly passed on, like a baton in a relay race. After Effective Communications, Ownership is easily the second most common factor in leadership. Think of all the situations in your daily life in which you've witnessed it, from something as simple as an incorrect order at a restaurant or as complex as a medical diagnosis where no one takes Ownership for their actions.

The importance of ownership became apparent to me early in my career, especially during my time in the US Air Force and while on assignment at the White House. From day one, the principle of ownership was drilled into everyone through training and protocol. It became second nature for me and those I worked with. If you have ownership of something, you have to deliver on that task or assignment until it is complete. If you need help, ask for it. If you see others needing assistance, help them. If you can't deliver on schedule, let your leader know and seek ways to remediate the situation. It is not acceptable to just fail and then miss an important delivery or deadline. If you own a piece of a larger process or system, deliver your piece until it is satisfactorily completed or taken on by someone else. I was fortunate enough to learn this by being in environments where failure was always possible but was never an option.

Today, we see public officials, politicians, and celebrities who are constantly trying to blame others for their own shortcomings and failures. It's a rare trait for someone famous to take ownership of a situation if it doesn't add to their material bottom line. Even more rare is to hear someone say, "I failed, but I learned from it and improved the next time." From my perspective, this failure to take ownership is a missed opportunity.

Often in internal meetings, on customer calls, and other business interactions (especially with email strings that go on forever), I'll ask, "Who owns this?" as it relates to next steps, moving things forward, improving a situation, or solving a problem. I find in many situations that failed actions or mistakes tend to be quickly divorced. As the old saying goes, "If everyone owns it, then no one owns it." It's an endemic problem in our business culture today, and even in our social culture.

Creating a culture of ownership in the workplace increases the likelihood of success and avoids delays, confusion, and failure. Document it, then inspect it and demand others do the same. A key factor in all of this is not to punish people for mistakes. Doing so creates a culture of fear. Fear destroys ownership.

Encourage ownership, allow people to learn from their mistakes, and document the process to avoid repeating the errors and to ensure replication of success. I have seen over and over again in my life, in my work, and in history that ownership leads to success and, conversely, lack of ownership leads to uncertainty and failure. Even if you do fail, you can always learn and grow.

Summary

It is almost a cliché in business to see business strategies depicted as houses or buildings. If you can imagine a graphic of such a building, there is a foundational layer with the core underpinnings of the operation. Then, there are at least three strategic pillars that stand atop the foundation. These are typically the means through which the business's objectives are realized. Finally, there is a roof covering it all, which is often the vision or mission. Pyramids are similar, with the added principle of strength which always hold up better than simply stacking blocks and having them fall down.

I have chosen a pyramid to illustrate the TTM Framework because that's how work is reflected in the real world. You have to have a broad foundation to hold the structure up. The central pieces are critical to the structural integrity of the model but can be switched out with some care. The topmost layers are the most flexible. You can get to them easily and exchange them out without too much risk of collapsing everything.

In TTM, your Core values will carry most of the weight of your leadership approach. They are absolutely essential and must be chosen and activated with the utmost care. In my experience Effective

Communication, Listening, and Ownership are the three principles that have been proven over and over again to mobilize teams and deliver results.

In the next chapter, we will examine aspects of the TTM Framework that are important, but which come with more flexibility.

> *"Things That Matter by Lonnie Essex is a practical, story-driven guide to leadership rooted in lived experience rather than theory...Through these stories, he distills ten Things That Matter that define his leadership approach. The book is refreshing because of its transparency. It is also inspiring and practical, reminding us that leadership is not about titles but about clarity, service, and authenticity. It challenges readers to define and live their own 'things that matter.'"*
>
> **Adrian Davis, President and CEO Whetstone Group, Inc. Author**

Chapter 3: Transformational and Aspirational TTM

Transformational TTM

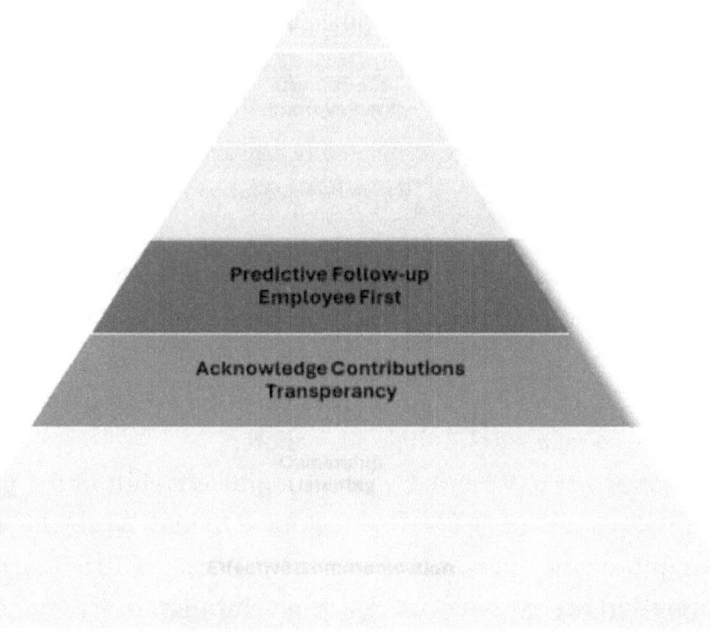

As I identified my personal Things That Matter, the Core items came intuitively. That is, they were the first items I thought of and required no deliberation or reflection. From my perspective, the three Core TTM which I have identified—Effective Communication, Listening, and Ownership—are the foundation for strong leadership. That is, for all leadership in all contexts in all situations. Throughout my life and career, I have witnessed the undeniably positive effects of these principles.

The four principles in the next layer of the TTM model are what I refer to as Transformational. My particular Transformational TTM:

- Transparency
- Acknowledge Contributions
- Employee First
- Predictive Follow-Up

All have made a significant impact on the quality of my leadership and the results that followed. I recognize, however, the relevance of these principles will vary according to context, such as industry, type of teams, and even the type of leadership one is engaged in. In general, Transformational TTM are more outwardly focused on others versus the Core TTM which are completely inwardly focused. You should master and own your Core TTM before moving to Transformational TTM.

Employee First, for instance, becomes more prominent when there is a clear delineation between employee and customer prioritization. In my experience, you can't have great customer service if your employees are unhappy. Quite simply, if you take care of your employees, they are more likely to take care of their customers.

It's important to note that there is a gradient shift in the principles as one moves up the TTM Framework Pyramid. With this in mind, let's explore the personal Transformational TTM that I have discovered in my experiences. As we go through these, I invite you to consider what Things That Matter may be transformational for you. As you review my personal TTM, think about your own and be ready for the steps later in the book that will guide you through developing your own set. Also, the TTM Role-Based Matrix illustrates how my personal TTM are applied to various situations and yours will too. It isn't a one-size-fits-all framework.

Lonnie's TTM	Work	Immediate Family	Extended Family	Friends	Mentor/ Coach
Effective Communication	☑	☑	☑	☑	☑
Listening	☑	☑	☑	☑	☑
Ownership	☑	☑	☑	☑	☑
Transparency	☑	☑	☑	☑	☑
Acknowledge Contributions	☑	☑	☑	☑	☑
Predictive Follow-up	☑				☑
Employee-First	☑				
Seeking Assistance	☑				☑
Continuous Improvement	☑	☑	☑		☑
Curiosity	☑	☑			☑

TM Role-Based Matrix

Transparency

Transparency, or what some may call honesty, integrity, and openness, lays the groundwork for trust in any relationship. Delivering on your commitments solidifies trust and creates an environment in which partnership can flourish.

In my experience, I have seen that all significant relationships, whether professional or personal, start with trust. Trust comes from consistently demonstrating honesty and openness and delivering on your commitments. It takes a fair amount of risk to do that. In personal relationships, you might call it vulnerability; in business, we call it transparency. As a leader, your actions will be magnified, whether good or bad—magnified and remembered. If others see you are willing to take the risk to be transparent about delivering on your commitments, trust will be earned.

An important truth to remember is that you can't force trust; it is always earned. When you have earned trust as a leader, your team, your employees, and your colleagues will listen to you more closely and will be willing to work with you toward your collective goals.

Many of the principles in my TTM are tightly related. Just like an actual pyramid, one building block depends on another. Pull one and the rest tumble down; reinforce one and the whole framework benefits. This is especially true of Effective Communication, Listening, and Transparency. <u>Effective Communication requires proper Listening and when you combine those two with Transparency that is when the magic really happens</u>. Employees contribute more discretionary effort, strategic objectives are delivered, and improvements are made to the bottom line. What's more, people can feel good about the mutually respectful way in which it was all done. Effective Communication, Listening, and Transparency cultivate engagement. Engagement, meaning that employees and team members feel invested in the organization and will therefore contribute more to achieving the common goals.

When I joined Unisys in 1997, I was the newly hired leader of a team of about 300 employees and contractors. What I said and what I did was recognized and followed by many others who, in turn, supported a wide range of customers. The initial number of 300, therefore, was magnified by the power of ten or more. I had to constantly be aware that the consequences of my words and actions could have a significant impact on our reputation and our results.

Within the team of 300, there was a nested team that supported a highly strategic customer. The problem was that the customer had become very dissatisfied. If that wasn't bad enough, the team that supported the customer felt demoralized. It was like a double-edged sword, and both edges, meaning success or failure, were exposed and sharp.

My first step, before I even met with the customer, was to let my team know that *together* we would make this situation better. To be clear, this wasn't a sunshine and puppies kind of meeting. We had to acknowledge our missteps—without casting blame and without burying ourselves in a hole of despair. I provided transparency on the problem, and I also provided transparency on the consequences of not resolving the problem.

Transparency is not always pretty, but if done right, it is always appreciated. Being transparent means being open and honest and sometimes the truth can hurt so it is important to be honest about the situation without causing others to feel offended. I insisted we take Ownership (TTM #3) of how we got there as well as how we were going to improve our situation. No one was going to fix this for us. Our organization and previous leadership had created the problem, and we had to fix it.

Once my team was aligned and committed with Employees First (TTM #6), my second step was to meet with the customer. In this meeting, I let the customer know we were committed to owning the issues and to rebuilding trust between their organization and our company. For me, this was not only a professional commitment but a personal one, especially as I had committed to my team that we would make this right.

To make a long story short, it took one meeting with the customer to convey our message of rebuilding trust and then about a year of hard, focused work to clearly deliver our promise in demonstrable, material ways. In that time, we made good on our word, and we earned back the trust we had lost. My team benefited and prospered, and we were recognized as the top team in the entire company (at the time a ~$7B gross revenue business).

In the following year, the customer became what we called a "reference account," which is a term meaning they helped us acquire new customers and expand our reach. We celebrated along the way, of course, rewarding top performers and incentivizing promising progress. It was great for the company, and that was part of it too, but mostly it was great for the team. The biggest reward was the sense of trust we developed not only with that key customer but within our own team and with our company. No one wanted to be working on a sinking ship.

As I look back, I realize that as the leader I had to set a new standard of performance and motivate my team to drive to that new standard. Effective Communication, Listening, and Ownership all played key roles, but Transparency with my team and the customer is what connected all the pieces.

Acknowledge Contributions

Everyone seeks to contribute meaningfully to a successful enterprise, be it a company, an event, a sports team, or a family unit. It's a natural human tendency. People want to contribute, and in turn they need to be acknowledged for those contributions. A great friend and colleague of mine often says, "Catch your employees doing something right and acknowledge them for it." I remind myself of this every day. You can say this in a million different ways—look for the positive, celebrate successes—I sum it up as simply as a TTM of Acknowledge Contributions. If you wait until success before acknowledging contributions, you may never arrive at success.

The best path to success is preparing the right person for the right role where they can deliver their best. Then, ensure they are trained and have repeatable processes and documented procedures to follow. Once you have the right people doing the right tasks with the right training and processes in place, you then need to support and encourage their success by acknowledging their contributions along the way. It's been my experience that without feedback loops in place to let employees know when they are doing well, they'll lose motivation or, worse, drift in the wrong direction.

Leaders are often too quick to point out errors or raise the alarm when something goes awry. It's tempting to do. It's also ineffective. The harder part is recognizing employees for doing the right things…even if you think it's self-evident. It's easy to focus only on mistakes and shortcomings, which is why so many people do it as it is part of human nature. Everyone has a story about a boss who lost their temper at the smallest of things. It's so common that people trade their stories like beads at Mardi Gras. What is much less common, rare even, are the stories about that one great boss who inspired and motivated, who made employees feel seen, and who acknowledged individual efforts. Many people have stories about those bosses, too, but they usually only have one. And that's a problem. As a leader, you must Acknowledge Contributions! You must be the leader that inspires and motivates employees and team members. This is a powerful way to lead, and the returns are immeasurable.

The way this is done looks different in every company and culture. Some organizations are able to build out formal rewards programs to incentivize small and large wins which tend to reward those in Sales but don't forget to recognize and reward other roles that were part of the success formula. More nimble organizations may have spot bonus programs, while others may rely on informal peer-to-peer recognition. For example, I've found that in the Middle East, employees love to be recognized in formal settings, with the all-important celebratory picture at the end with their boss. In other cultures, a quiet, non-public acknowledgement may be preferred. Monetary compensation is important to a lot of people, but you'll also find that many just want their good work to be noticed and to be recognized. Not to make it overly complicated, but every person has their own preferred way to be recognized, and your job as a leader is to discover their preference by Listening (TTM #2).

Employee First

For years, companies have chanted the mantra of "customer first." Sometimes they mean it; sometimes they don't. From my perspective, it's a marketing ploy. Take, for instance, self-checkout machines. Retailers, grocers, and fast-food chains say they do this for their customers. The theory is that it improves customer experience by reducing check-out times and adding capacity. I'll pause right there as your pulse rate escalates.

The truth is that the primary driver for self-checkout machines is to reduce labor costs. Technology is expensive, but smart retailers can take advantage of advances in technology tools that are more productive and efficient especially with almost daily advances with AI. Compare that to a human cashier, who needs an array of benefits, not to mention actual wages, time off, pay raises, and overtime. When you do the analysis, it's clear that self-checkout machines are there for the company and not the customer. They may cut costs and be more productive and efficient, but the customer experience unravels quickly when you're at that machine and you didn't weigh your apples or something doesn't scan. Suddenly, you're now working for the retailer, and you didn't even apply for the job!

I realized after years of hearing companies say, "The customer always comes first," that as a leader when you put your employees and teammates first, they in turn will provide better service and support to your customers. This doesn't mean that the customers aren't important. It just means that for many reasons if we are leading others in any role to achieve a common goal, we need to treat our people like they matter—remunerate them well, give them good benefits, and treat them like actual human beings. I learned this the hard way, and thankfully I course-corrected before I did too much damage.

All leaders have blind spots and one for me was "tough love." People used to call me "the Intimidator" due to my tough leadership style. Sadly, I was actually proud of that term at the time before I matured as a leader and as a person five to six years later. I saw something ugly in myself, and it was doing no one any good. I also learned that putting employees first also means preparing them to succeed. This is done by providing tangible support such as meaningful training, coaching, development, tools, resources and intangibles such as inspiration, understanding, and, yes, Listening. You have to genuinely care about their well-being and their success and demonstrate that at a level that everyone can see, including your customers. This can occur even by leaders who are introverts with the right TTM.

Many years ago, as a regional general manager I ran a technology division for my company. At the time, it was a typical dilemma to never have enough resources, especially during project surges. Every business in every industry will face this. Customers especially want your "best people" on their projects. This becomes a real problem when project schedules collide, and you're faced with difficult prioritization choices: *Which customer or project gets the resources and when?*

My organization was overseeing literally hundreds of simultaneous customer projects when we ran into one of these project surges. I had a very large and important customer who was building a new headquarters facility locally, and my company was fortunate to be responsible for certain technological components of this new construction project. As the overall project was facing larger delays with other contributing aspects, we were asked to compensate for any schedule delays by accelerating when we could. We did this until we got to the point where there were so many large delays across the entire spectrum of the wider project—e.g. far out of my control and not even within our company's remit—that no matter what we did, we could never make up for the gap. There simply were not enough resources. We were running at full capacity with no reserves to spare.

We made the only sensible decision we could under the circumstances. We would let the other work streams who held our interdependencies catch up and then we could resume where we left off. In the meantime, our resources were moved to other important projects and/or were given some much-deserved time off.

When the Chief Information Officer (CIO) from the customer caught wind of this sequencing, they complained to our CEO. Upon our CEO's request, I met with the CIO and explained everything that my company and team had done to accelerate, making it clear that we could only do so much to make up for the shortfalls of others. Despite the discussion, the CIO demanded my team should work over another holiday weekend. If nothing else, the CIO felt the optics would be good—that is, we would demonstrate commitment, and that might inspire others regardless of the fact that it would have little to no measurable impact.

I explained that my employees had families and needed time off to recharge. If I, as the leader, didn't ensure the well-being of my team, then they wouldn't be able to deliver their best. I was clear that I had to put my employees and their lives and families first so they could do their jobs well for our customers. The CIO didn't like this at first, but he eventually relented and even admitted he saw the wisdom in it.

After the holiday weekend, my team came back rested and motivated. The project still faced other delays, but it concluded successfully. When the site opened, we had a ribbon-cutting celebration, and the CIO was more than pleased with the results.

Sometimes putting Employees First is about implementing a policy or listening before acting. On a daily basis, as leaders we're faced with making decisions both large and small concerning competing priorities. Do we put the investors first, the customers, our employees, costs, revenues? This is the reality of leading a team in business. These conflicts are real, and they come up often. We start with driving results, of course, and deliver on our commitments, but we also have to remember that if we always put our customers first, then our employees may suffer, which will have a negative impact on the overall endeavor. Having a clear understanding of our Things That Matter can serve as a compass. As a hint, employees always matter.

Predictive Follow-Up

Predictive follow-up is about anticipating with a high degree of accuracy what is likely to go wrong and taking measures to avoid it. The term mixes the forward-facing concept of 'predictive' with the reactive concept of 'follow-up.' Predictive Follow-up involves anticipating controllable circumstances and taking proactive measures before they happen. This can also be called planning for failure. Most of the time we do well planning for success. When do we ever plan for failure?

I learned the value of this principle in a way that was both unusual and unfortunate. As a young leader in my late twenties, I started out charging hard. I cringe to say it now, but I was unnecessarily harsh at times. I'm not sure where I got it from, but I felt that to get things done I had to crack down on myself and others. I had a very short tolerance for mistakes.

I was overseeing a large project for a very important customer, which involved the international shipment of critical components. My teammate was responsible for logistics. Well, we all know about logistics and just how easily things can get knocked off track by anything from inclement weather to transport disruptions to tie-ups with customs. If it is going by air, there will be airport closures; if it is going by sea, there will be port issues. Logistics is the one area where if anything can go wrong, it will. And in this case, it did. In brief, the shipment was significantly delayed, which then caused the entire project to slip and traveling teams to be impacted.

The customer was disappointed, my teammate was devastated, and I was furious. I had no filter and a bad sense of timing. I expressed my displeasure to my colleague in front of a number of people. I regretted it the moment I did it, but once the words were let loose, there was no taking them back. They took it badly, as anyone would. As a leader, I was deeply ashamed of my behavior, and I did what I could to make amends. We were able to get the project back on track, and I learned a hard lesson.

Hard lesson number one was about treating colleagues and employees with respect. That became an entire element unto itself in my Things That Matter, which is Employees First. The other was about avoiding things you know are likely to go wrong. As noted, logistics is always a choke point in any project's critical path. Instead of scolding my colleague after the fact, I should have made sure that we had contingencies built into our plan to cover for an inevitable shipment delay. I should have predicted and followed up with viable solutions.

On a smaller scale, I often see employees struggle with hard-to-reach clients. I recently had a project manager come to me in desperation saying, "I can't get the customer to respond to me. They asked me to get this done by next week, and I'm trying to communicate with them so we can schedule and organize, but they won't respond!"

My response was, "Well, that's going to happen. It's always going to happen. They're going to say, 'This is urgent. I need it.' Then they're going to go dark on you." Customers have many other priorities as well, so know that they are likely as busy as you are trying to keep up with their responsibilities.

I then explained that we should ask the customer for the best time and method to contact them (call, email, text, Slack, WhatsApp, etc.). Always have multiple contacts, multiple ways to get in touch with our customer or someone close to them, because the moment we're single-threaded like that—meaning the customer is the single point of accountability—we're in trouble when the contact becomes unavailable for whatever reason. That's predictable. That's always going to happen. Get ready for it. The follow-up is clear: have more than one way to contact that person or insist on a suitable delegate—before it becomes a problem. We can't be surprised when what we know is going to happen, happens. Plan for it.

Aspirational TTM

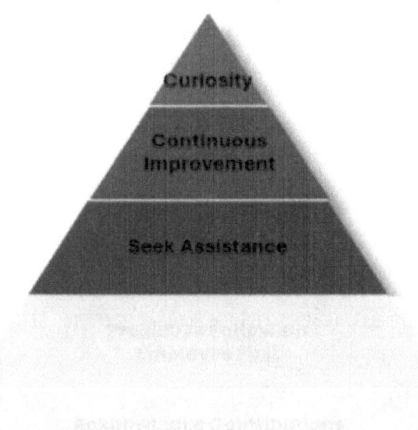

This portion of the TTM Framework Pyramid comprises Aspirational principles. These should be considered completely flexible. Aspirational TTM should be wholly dependent on one's personal experiences and preferences. They should also be "stretch targets"; that is, principles which you strongly believe in but which you are still working on. Often, Aspirational TTM come to us later in our careers, whereas Core and Transformational may be there right from the beginning.

Seek Assistance

Throughout my career and my personal life, I have found that people are afraid to Seek Assistance. I'm not sure if it is a Western problem or a global problem. Perhaps it's generational. In companies, sometimes it's a simple matter that the organizational culture doesn't support it. Most performance management systems reward employees based on individual contributions. They have objectives, targets, and measures to indicate how well they did. In such a system, no one wants to even hint they might need assistance in any area; it's like admitting failure or incompetence. It seems like a fast track to a low rating. The truth is the exact opposite.

In an environment in which everyone is afraid to ask for help, there are going to be gaps, serious gaps. And not just with one employee, but systemic. In such workplaces, we're going to miss things, a lot of things. If we foster an environment where employees and even leaders themselves can ask for help and actually get it, that's an environment that fosters growth and success.

My motto is "Don't suffer in silence." Too many times, when someone doesn't quite understand what needs to be done, they clam up. The problem could be with a particular way to run an analysis, or maybe it's just how to initiate a procurement request. Maybe it wasn't part of the onboarding. Maybe management assumed that *everyone* knew the process simply because *someone* knew the process. The individual is thinking if they just had a little input from someone else, or if there was a desk procedure, they could solve the problem. In these situations, I encourage my team to speak up, to seek assistance. "Let us know. Let's not fail." "If we do fail, we fail together."

We operate in a world where profit margins are always tough to maintain. Any industry that has a strong sense of competition is going to have thinner profit margins. And when margins are thin, there's never going to be enough resources regardless of how much volume is coming through. Whether it's people, capital and revenue, or time, there's never enough because there isn't enough gross profit to go around to fund everything that's needed. Even if there was, another company would be more efficient, and resources would have to be trimmed to effectively compete.

As leaders, we always have to get by with what we have. Meaning, deal with the situation as it is and not the way we want it to be with more resources and more budget. I learned that simple lesson in my household growing up. We had limited resources. No one was going to wave a magic wand and suddenly double or triple our income. If we wanted something, we'd have to figure out how to stretch what we had to get it. My father would never have asked for or accepted handouts but there were many in the community that helped us in other ways, keep in mind how generous my father was to others in their time of need. Intentionally or not, my father had created a culture of reciprocity, which is perhaps the core definition of community.

This same principle applies in the workplace. As an example, let's say we have a large capital project that needs ten engineers. Due to budget and headcount restraints, however, we only have six engineers available for the job. We do our best work with those six. But then, as usually happens in these cases, those six engineers doing the work of ten ran into some very real hurdles. They might get overwhelmed with the workload, maybe the deadlines have been moved up, maybe the customer changed their specs. They can't do it all. Instead of raising their hand and saying, "Hey, I can't get all this done. Can we have some assistance?" they keep quiet. They miss key milestones, the project gets delayed, the customer is unhappy, and the team gets demoralized. Less than satisfactory results all the way around.

Why does this happen? Maybe the team doesn't want to be seen as complainers, maybe they think management won't budge, maybe they can't see an obvious solution. And what could be done? Perhaps some engineers could be shifted from other projects, deadlines renegotiated, priorities re-stacked. As the saying goes, you don't know what you don't know—but we will never know the answers to either of these questions unless someone first Seeks Assistance.

The key point is that as a leader, we have to create an environment for our employees and teams to know it is okay to Seek Assistance. When a leader creates a culture of reciprocity, people lose their fear of asking for help. Not surprisingly, in such an environment, people are also more willing to assist, and the team's collective ability to succeed increases.

Continuous Improvement

The idea of Continuous Improvement has been around for a very long time, longer than the 1950s, when most researchers cite its emergence following WWII. What surfaced at that time was largely focused on gaining incremental improvements, especially process-related, in manufacturing. That concept, of course, can be easily applied to all areas of business and life and, in that sense, it far outdates even the industrial revolution. One could argue it's as old as humankind. But as ubiquitous as it may be in our history, it's woefully absent in our everyday practices. Many would rather settle back into an unwavering routine of ineffectiveness than face the prospect of change.

I maintain that a good leader should continuously strive for enhanced productivity and efficiency in every task and process. They should look for ways to automate tasks and improve support for their teams. I realized this first when I joined the US Air Force in 1982. With every assignment and job I have taken since then, it has always been apparent to me that the need to continually improve is essential to the mission and the organization as a whole.

The world is becoming difficult to predict and increasingly competitive. That's the nature of business. With every new start-up, spin-off, joint venture, or product line, every industry in every market is becoming more challenging, with tighter margins requiring leaner organizations with more efficient processes. Customers and shareholders also add pressure to the already intense environment, expecting more for their investments. In this type of ruthless ecosystem, if you aren't improving, you're moving backwards. History is filled with failed leviathans who thought they were too big to fail…until they inevitably did.

During my tenure at Cisco, for several years I was a leader in the Channels organization. There, I managed a series of large global partners. One of the things we looked at was their metrics from an outside-in point of view. This meant we would have them surveyed and look at not just how we measured them, but how they felt about their partnership with us. We could always look at our own metrics and tell a story from that perspective, but we wanted to know our partners' perspective. Were they satisfied? Did we meet their expectations?

I recall one particular instance when it became apparent that our partners felt like we as a company needed to do more to help them. This was a tremendous wake-up call for us. If we just went by our key performance indicators, we would have said everything was good, in fact, more than good. But our partners thought otherwise. And if your partners (who were essentially customers) aren't happy, they aren't likely to be your customers for long.

We ended up redesigning our channel program for services. This was no small undertaking. It required a significant amount of change. There were those who didn't want to do things differently. They thought the way we always did things was good enough. They pointed to our internal KPIs as evidence. But according to our customers, we weren't looking at the right things. Or perhaps we were, but the targets had moved. The customers had higher expectations because the market itself had become more competitive. Our current approach may have been good yesterday, but it was struggling to chin the bar today and certainly wouldn't tomorrow.

We course-corrected. It wasn't easy. It required a change of mindset, which then led to improved processes and systems as well as new channel programs, metrics, and incentives. It was an avalanche of change once we got started, but instead of potential destruction, we reaped results. One of the things we did was to pull our partners together and conduct a rather simple exercise. I should say the exercise itself is simple, but following through on the action items that came out of the exercise wasn't so simple.

We conducted a straightforward "stop, start, continue" exercise. We asked our partners a series of key questions: what are we doing that we should stop? What should we start doing? What's working that we should continue doing?

The answers we received were overwhelming in volume but insightful in quality. We immediately began instituting improvements that yielded strong results and kept our customers happy, profitable, and able to compete.

We did this many years ago. I have long since left Cisco, but I expect they haven't stood still. I expect the programs we implemented then to have been improved step-by-step, year-on-year. Because that's what has to be done to stay in the game. Anyone who wants to sit down should take their place on the sidelines where they can watch the game go on without them. I say "game" as a metaphor. It's a useful and simple analogy. Our business and our lives, however, aren't games, which makes the case for a Continuous Improvement mindset all the more important.

Curiosity

The last principle in my TTM Framework Pyramid is Curiosity. Its place on the list doesn't mean that it's the least important. In fact, since it tops off the whole pyramid, it acts as the capstone, providing essential structural integrity. I have found that Curiosity is a key problem-solving skill and a way to learn new things. If you don't have this skill, I encourage you to develop it.

As an example, when AI became widely accessible, many people ran in fear. "It will never last," they said. "It is one step too far! It's counterproductive. It's just a fad." Early adopters who were curious to learn more about the technology were seen as heretics. Today, those same heretics have progressed from early adopters to champions of a game-changing innovation. Their peers, who mocked them, are struggling to catch up. This is just a simple recent example of the benefits of curiosity. Curiosity, in many ways, is a business fundamental.

When I interview candidates for any position, I pose the following scenario: *Give me an example of how you used your curiosity to solve a customer request or problem.*

Usually, I'm met with a moment of silence as the candidate gathers their thoughts. I can almost hear the hinges squeaking as they open door after door in their memory for a suitable experience to retell. And by the way, this pause in no way counts against them. To me, it indicates I've triggered some deep thinking, and I am happy to wait for the results.

Usually, a confident expression will cross the candidate's face as a story dawns on them and they see the pathway open. The candidate will then lean into their story, explaining the problem, explaining their seemingly unorthodox approach to a solution that they discovered through serendipitous curiosity. I love these moments. Through their answers, I learn about the candidate's ability to learn and grow and their desire to discover new things. To me, it reveals not only a healthy habit of inquisitiveness, their ability to sell complex solutions and solve complex challenges, but it also indicates that they're teachable and coachable. This is the type of employee I'm always looking for. Of course, there are other qualifications needed, both technical and behavioral, but from my experience, Curiosity is the true indicator of future success.

I've talked a lot about business in this chapter. Things That Matter, however, has a place in all aspects of one's life. Curiosity is one such principle. Genealogical research has turned into a life passion for me. As I shared, my parents passed away when I was very young. Three of my four grandparents also passed away by the time I was thirteen. My last grandparent passed away when I was in my early twenties.

Maybe it's because of these losses that I have found myself looking for a connection to my past. When I was in my forties, it all caught up with me. I thought to myself, "I have no idea where I came from. I know nothing about my ancestors. Where do I come from? Really."

My curiosity prompted me to research my ancestry. Thankfully, with so many great resources out there today, genealogical research is much easier than it ever has been. The more my Curiosity pushed me, the more I dug and the more I found.

Now, after more than a decade, having spent literally thousands of hours on research, I have amassed a treasure trove of data that can live forever. In my personal family tree, I have over 4,000 documented ancestors and relatives. I have searched every bloodline as far back as possible. One bloodline goes back through several royal ancestors as far back as the third century AD (~1,800 years ago!). I have seventeen documented ancestors who were patriots in the American/British Revolutionary War. I have ancestors that served in the War of 1812, the US Civil War, and many others. I have been accepted into several royal and ancestral societies such as: The Baronial Order of Magna Charta, The Military Order of Crusades, and recently The Descendants of Templar Knights by proving connection to prominent ancestors all dating back almost 1,000 years. I now write short stories for my family about our history and help others in their own genealogical quests. Curiosity has opened so many doors for me, in my work and my personal life and it can do the same for you.

Summary

As I wrote this book, I was challenged to consider if my Things That Matter would apply to others in whole or in part. That maybe I could shorten this book by half if I just said, "These are my Things That Matter. They should matter to you too. Take them, live them, and prosper."

But I can't do that. Because I don't believe that.

As my model supports, I believe that some Things That Matter are Core, some Transformational, and some Aspirational. While I would like to believe that a person would do well from adopting all of my own Things That Matter, I recognize that in doing so they would have to disregard some of their own Things That Matter. So, my practical guide will walk you through how to create your own TTM.

Each person gathers lessons and principles throughout the course of their lives through their own unique experiences. I have asked colleagues, friends, mentees, and family to share with me their Things That Matter. For the many who shared them, I have been delighted to find how they differ from my own. Especially if they didn't know mine at first. Often, there have been overlaps, and these delight me as well. What always differs, though, are the experiences and reasons that these friends, colleagues, and family members believe what they believe.

There is always a story, always a revelatory insight behind each TTM. And when they shared their TTMs, that's what I treasure the most.

In the following chapter, we will delve into ways that you, can discover and create your own Things That Matter. Once we have covered how to discover and document Things That Matter, we will then explore the process of communicating and then living your Things That Matter. I promise you it is a simple process. I also promise you that it is a challenging process. Above all, I promise it will be immensely rewarding and will ultimately benefit you and all those around you in business and life.

> *"Sitting down to read "Things That Matter" is like having a conversation with Lonnie Essex, my mentor. This book is not just a list of tips for success; it reveals the authentic leadership principles that Essex uses to coach others. These lessons resonate because it's clear that this is how he coaches himself; he truly lives it...For anyone aspiring to become a more effective leader, this book offers genuine insights into how to identify and commit to the actions required for growth. In work and in life, growth is only embodied if it first aligns with our "Things That Matter."*
>
> **Kelly Dias, Director of Sales, AVI-SPL**

Chapter 4: Discovering Our Things That Matter

Socrates is often attributed with saying, "Know thyself," though variations of the aphorism are known to pre-date him. Plato, a student of Socrates, reinterpreted the maxim to mean, broadly, "know your soul." Regardless of its history, it remains one of the hardest tenets to master. There's something about introspection that makes it both accessible yet elusive. Identifying our own Things That Matter is similar—it's the simplest thing we can do, but at the same time one of the hardest.

On the one hand, how could we not know what things matter to us? We have lived with ourselves our entire lives. On the other hand, not many people have taken the time to ask themselves this simple question of "what things matter to me." Life, after all, can be very busy. Each minute seems to be filled with a myriad of shiny distractions bombarding us at every turn. Taking a few hours to sort through our priorities is a lot less compelling than doomscrolling on social media (like Instagram, TikTok, X, etc.)...but it's a lot healthier!

Identifying our personal Things That Matter is a discovery process. Like an actual discovery, for some it may come as quick and easy as following a hunch; for others it may require careful introspection, earnest deliberation, and lots of trial and error. It all depends on how we as individuals are wired. The best approach, as is often the case, is a hybrid, balancing the two tactics, relying first on intuition and then testing the results with honest reflection.

Creating a Template

Let's begin at the beginning. Always a good place to start! Since 2004, I have been a mentor and coach in a formal professional capacity and informal personal settings. It's a role I enjoy—passing on lessons I've learned, helping others to gain perspective on their individual circumstances and to identify possible paths forward. To be honest, I also learn from the people I mentor. If done right, mentoring is never a one-way street. Both parties walk away with a little more insight into their motivations, their options, and, most importantly, themselves.

During the process of mentoring, the topic of Things That Matter invariably arises. In fact, it is one of the first things I ask: *What are the Things That Matter to you? Have you thought about that? Can you take some time to think about it and come back to me with a list of four or five things?*

I ask this to get a baseline of the person's self-knowledge and to understand where they're coming from. It's been my experience that the first step in figuring out where we're going is to determine where we've been. Unsurprisingly, not a single person I have ever asked this question has answered in the affirmative. Some people have thought about these questions, sure, but no one has ever sat down and documented them in a format they could refer to or even share with others. When we explore this idea, though, they are usually excited to take on the challenge and often ask me about mine, which I'm happy to share.

As you can imagine, this tends to lead to rich discussions. People want to know why I chose my items and how I use them. Some also want to adopt them as their own, which I always caution against. I firmly believe each person should have their own Things That Matter based on their own experiences and own beliefs. Of course, there is nothing wrong if some items end up being similar. Effective Communication, for instance, is a ubiquitous trait that one would expect to see as a high priority for most people unless they are introverted. There is a danger, however, in adopting someone else's complete roster of Things That Matter as one's own. I encourage my mentees to think about their own experiences and to choose mentors and role models that can help shape them, and figure out what is truly important.

Netting It Out

I often get into discussions with my mentees about what exactly I mean by Things That Matter. In these cases, the mentee might ask me to define it precisely. Are we talking about values, principles, or convictions? Should we think about them in the context of our personal lives or the workplace? (If there is even a difference between the two anymore with work-life integration!)

These are all legitimate questions that deserve thoughtful answers. As noted, one of my Things That Matter is Curiosity. I became curious to learn more about the nuances and differences of terms such as values and beliefs, convictions, morals, principles. When I spoke about Things That Matter, was I really just talking about convictions or values or any of the other terms? How did they differ? How were they alike?

In Greek tradition, hydras were fearsome mythical beasts with multiple heads, usually five to seven. Hercules, as part of his twelve labors, had to combat a hydra. To his consternation, he discovered that if he chopped off one head, two more would grow in its place. My investigation into the meaning of these terms had similar results; that is, when I looked up one term, six more would pop up, each with its own meanings and connotations.

For instance, some reference materials indicate that 'principles' are universal, objective, and, most importantly, external. Gravity, for example, is a principle. 'Values,' in contrast, are internal and subjective, and are based on a person's own experiences. 'Convictions,' however, are more about the classification of right and wrong. Then there are 'beliefs' and 'standards' and 'tenets'…it just goes on and on. To be honest, I was a bit overwhelmed. Was my idea of Things That Matter really so complicated?

I thought back to my military days. The military, for all its supposed bureaucracy, had a way of dealing with complexity. I characterize it as "netting it out." In my military assignments, we frequently had to push things up the chain of command to the appropriate level of authority to make needed decisions. This is common practice in most corporations as well. Delegations of authority make it clear who can decide on what, depending on areas of remit, costs, or ramifications. To make sound decisions, my superiors needed the right information—not every minute detail, but a summary of key information. I quickly developed the ability to net things out; meaning, I learned to assess complex situations, gather the relevant facts and details, and then concisely summarize them in a short document or briefing.

A useful way to report status is by using two categories: "What's Ready and Up and What's Not Ready." We frequently used this in the military to provide quick and constant updates. Instead of struggling to filter through data and information, we simply asked ourselves, "What's ready and what's not ready?" While working at the White House, if we were awaiting a presidential arrival to an event, location, or venue, we only had to indicate up the chain of command, "Ready to Receive." This was the entire status report to senior officials—that for our area of responsibility we were ready to receive the President or other senior White House Staff.

After my tour at the White House, I was assigned to the US Air National Guard in a Combat Communications unit outside the nation's capital. I typically ran the Operations Center for the unit and while deployed would often report our unit's status in the same manner. It worked and worked well. The military and the federal government in general very commonly net things out. Briefings are called that for a reason; they should be literally "brief" and to the point!

I carried this skill with me after the military, and I still very much use it today. In business, I tend to think along the same lines for sales or operations when reporting up-channel. For sales, it's always "What's in and what's left?" as it relates to managing a sales forecast. For operations, it's always "What's done and what remains?" and "How much budget is expended and how much budget remains?" It's the same repeatable process to net things out quickly and to be crisp around Effective Communication. Over the years I have found this a pragmatic and simple way to defragment complicated issues, especially with higher-level executives and leaders as well as with partners and customers.

And so, as I faced the metaphorical hydra in trying to precisely define the concept of Things That Matter, as I pondered over the questions "Are Things That Matter values, principles, or convictions? Are they beliefs, standards, tenets or maybe something else entirely?" I took a step back and netted it out. My answer to these questions is simply "yes." Yes, Things That Matter can be principles, values, convictions...so long as they actually matter to you and so long as you consistently live into them, demonstrating them in your daily behaviors in both large and small ways. When you net it out, when you consolidate all the theory and nuance into something that is relevant and usable, Things That Matter is really as simple as it sounds. Similarly, the process of discovering them is also simple. Let's begin with three steps to discover your TTM.

- Step 1: Write First, Edit Later
- Step 2: Internal and External Validation
- Step 3: Maintain and Sustain

Step 1: Write First, Edit Later

My Things That Matter came about organically; that is, over time they grew and developed through a sort of incubation process. By the time I recognized the need to articulate them, I had about six or seven items clearly identified, and I could express them verbally or in written format very quickly. Once I committed them to paper, which was early 2020, once I had them in a format that I could look at and then put away and then come back to, only then could I really examine and interrogate them.

Step 1, therefore, is to simply sit down and write out four or five Things That Matter to you. Don't overthink this step. Being intuitive means trusting your instincts. This very first step merely involves committing your ideas to paper (or screen). Ask yourself the questions based on "how you feel." Start with one to three words. For example, if you feel Authenticity is one of your Things That Matter, you can write that single word or you might expand it slightly, e.g., *represent myself honestly*.

If you find yourself stumped at four or five items, don't fret. The next stage of the process will begin to loosen up the gravel, so to speak. You may find that some of your terms comprise two or more concepts. Or in examining one, you may recollect others. The point is, try not to become frustrated if you don't feel you have enough items. More will come. Also, it is good to seek input from your trusted advisors. How do they see you and how do they feel about your TTM? In fact, since I always think about my TTM, when I meet someone new and they tell me about themselves I can usually listen and playback what sounds like some of their things that matter. I usually say "it sounds like some of your things that matter are family, helping others, etc." As you mature in life you will have more TTM, and some will change so plan to continue the process for life.

Similarly, don't worry if you find you have exceeded four or five. As they say, "Too much is always enough." In these cases, you are likely to find that you can consolidate items. Sometimes ideas can be so important to you that you inadvertently restate them several times using different phrasing. The target number you are looking for is ten, with a range of eight to twelve.

In a world of no guarantees, I can guarantee your initial list of Things That Matter will neither be complete nor final. You will add some; you will delete others. What you are convinced is correct today is likely to change tomorrow. And that is okay. The trick is to get something down on paper.

Some people prefer to write out a quick list and then cycle back to the top once they have exhausted their ideas. At that point, they flesh out each word or phrase more fully. Others may choose to take on each one as they come up. Either approach is fine. Follow the method that is most comfortable with your particular thinking process. Mileage will vary for introverts and extraverts. We are all different.

Next, for each item you have written, expand your thinking into one to three sentences. As you do this, read back over your sentences and think about each word. Here, it is okay to let your linguistic hydra loose. Think about feelings, capture them in words, and then re-examine them. Keep in mind that what you are looking to capture is what the term or phrase means to you, not to Merriam-Webster or Wikipedia, but you. You are defining these terms based on your experiences, behaviors, and preferences. As an example, if Authenticity is one of your terms, ask yourself how you personally define it and exemplify it.

At the point at which you are expanding and refining your terms, you have entered the questioning stage. This is where the real fun starts! As you go through this process, you'll notice several things. One is that several of your items may be very similar to others on your list. If so, you may choose to combine them, shifting how you characterize them, making them more precise or even more general.

Second, you're likely to notice that many are interrelated. This is natural. We all tend to operate in self-contained systems, which thrive on internal consistency. We human beings naturally seek harmony between our thoughts, values, and actions. That's how humans make sense of the world and of themselves. If you notice you have several items that are closely interwoven, you may want to consider if they are actually part of a larger concept. Like a cell phone camera, you can easily zoom in or out on your ideas. For me, one of my TTMs is Transparency (TTM #4). This covers a lot of territory like trust, integrity, honesty, respect, and potentially more, but I had to define that in my process of netting out all of my initial thoughts. Remember, this isn't a test, and there are no wrong answers. Only you defining you!

On my website at LonnieEssex.com, you will find the "Subset of TTM Table." It will show you my finished product, which includes my ten TTM plus sub-categories of other things that fit under each of the TTM. Don't worry if you don't get to this quickly, as it took years for me to get to sub-categories. However, if you happen to have a lot of interrelated TTM, it may be a way for you to consolidate, so please use the Subset of TTM Table as an example if it helps you!

Once you are satisfied with your first draft, be it four or twelve items, put the list away for at least a day to incubate, or if you prefer cooking metaphors, to marinate. If you have immediate changes, or if something dawns on you that you don't want to forget, it's okay to return to the list to make the amendments. In doing so, don't be surprised if you're drawn back into the process. Developing your first draft, or your first extended draft, can be a tricky task. Regardless of how many times you return to it, try to walk away for at least twenty-four hours once the compulsion to edit has simmered down. It is important to also imagine what happens if your TTM did not exist and how it may affect your life.

Returning to the draft after twenty-four hours, you'll have a refreshed perspective. Read through the list from beginning to end, and make the necessary additions, deletions, and changes as needed. I caution my mentees to use version control; that is, number each significant draft. Often you may decide the previous way you worded something might be better than the latest version you edited yourself into. It's always handy to go back and refer to previous drafts. With your second and subsequent versions, you are refining your ideas to a stable iteration that you can share with others. Once you get to this version, you have completed the first step.

Step 2: Internal and External Validation

With your stable draft of eight to twelve Things That Matter, you're ready to move on to internal and external validation. In this step, you'll test your ideas with yourself and with others. I have learned the hard way that a key step in building a business case, plan, or project is to state and test key assumptions. There is nothing worse than embarking on a large capital project only to discover key factors like the cost of goods or the accessibility of talent are incorrect! In this stage, what you are doing is validating the assumptions you have of yourself and, as in most solid evaluations, you need both internal and external perspectives.

Be honest with yourself. There is no reason to exaggerate or especially to be dishonest. As an example, this will be discovered if you say that one of your TTMs is "honesty" and you are known as a dishonest person. You'll likely get the "double eye roll." You need to be very honest with yourself, with no exaggeration. Now, some of your Aspirational TTM can be things that are important to you and that you are still working on, but they should all be in the realm of what identifies you. While writing this book, I asked several friends and family to go through this very process. The results were very affirmative. Each person's TTM list clearly and easily identified them as others see them and as they see themselves. Success!

Internal validation involves yet more introspection. For each item and description, create several sub-bullets of proof points. Ask yourself in what specific instances you have found yourself demonstrating the noted idea. If you find yourself struggling to find an appropriate example, then ask if the concept is right or try to dig deeper. If you are stuck, you may want to go on to the next item and return later.

As you write out your proof-points, try to capture the essential details. When did it happen? Who was involved? What was the outcome? Shoot for the magic number of three details. One is interesting, two is a coincidence; three is a pattern. Also, try to steer away from crafting a journal entry or long narrative. While these may be worthwhile efforts, the point here is to stand up your list in a fairly short space of time.

An important thing to remember when you develop your list is that it is not going to come out fully formed and perfect. You may find you have gaps in your growing list—one or two proof points missing here and there. This is okay. The validation process will not only help to test your initial list, but it will help to fill in gaps.

Once you have thoroughly cycled through your list at least once, it's time to socialize the content. There is a strong possibility that socializing will either cause you to remember more, or the person you share them with may actually provide some additional detail. When I was first building my initial list, I recall sharing it with my close family and several close subordinate managers. I even shared it with a few people whom I considered my mentors. It was a type of sanity check on what I had written and how they would be received. While I was confident in what I had committed to in writing, I was less confident that I genuinely showed up that way. Sure, I knew I believed in these things, but would the people that knew me and saw me in action on a day-to-day basis see me the same way?

We tend to think the best of ourselves. It's a natural tendency. Another natural tendency is to shy away from evidence suggesting we aren't as great as we thought. One of the leaders I worked with had an expression, "Feedback is the Breakfast of Champions" which is so true so accept it and learn from it. And so, when I shared that first list, I took a deep breath and braced for the feedback. I was pleasantly surprised, however, with the results—not that everyone agreed with every word, but in the quality of input I received. With that input, I was able to take a more honest assessment of myself, which was a tremendous help in honing my initial Things That Matter.

This can be a scary step for some people. Sharing your Things That Matter involves risk and vulnerability. The person or persons you choose to share your Things That Matter with, therefore, should be someone you trust, someone who knows you in the context you have used, and someone who will be honest in their reflections. If you expect to grow as a person, you need to open yourself up to understanding how others perceive you. It is so valuable to the development process, in fact, that many companies institute formal feedback programs to provide important insights into their leadership about how they come across to others.

The feedback process can involve surveying people above, below, and lateral to the subject person, asking questions relevant to key areas such as leadership skills, collaboration, decision making, and more. It also collects the individuals' view of themselves.

Once all the responses are collected, collated, and analyzed, the leader is briefed on the results, often directly with their teams. A professional facilitator helps them dig into the results and surface important factors. I've known many people who thought they were great at teamwork only to discover that is not how others perceived them. I have also known people who underestimated how strong they were in certain areas that they thought they were weak in.

While I am not suggesting everyone needs a formal assessment to validate their Things That Matter, feedback mechanisms can be a valuable resource to test one's assumptions about how they show up to others as well as a source for proof points.

Whether you use a formal feedback tool or do it through informal means, when you share your Things That Matter, be sure to ask for reactions at two levels:

1. Is your case stated clearly; meaning, does what you say make sense in all the ways you meant it to make sense? This will require some discussion. It is certainly appropriate to email your list to the person in mind, but make sure you have a conversation about the material as well so you can check for understanding and provide additional context as needed.
2. Does the material ring as true? Has the person seen you demonstrate this behavior? Could they have predicted it would end up on your list simply because that is the way you truly are? Don't be disappointed if others don't see you as you see yourself. This is valuable information. It indicates that there is a misalignment between what you think and how you act and

tells you to adjust one or the other. This identifies a potential blind spot, which is important feedback to have on your development and leadership journey.

Going through this process will allow you to fine-tune your Things That Matter. It may also spark thoughts around new items. Both of these outcomes are appropriate and rewarding. At this stage, you'll want to update your list to reflect your new perspective and move on to Step 3 of the documentation stage—Maintain and Sustain.

Step 3: Maintain and Sustain

Compared to Steps 1 and 2, Step 3 is perhaps the easiest—though it is also the longest. In this step, you're going to maintain your list by reviewing it periodically and updating it as needed. Don't be discouraged if your list changes and evolves over time—it should. As you garner more experiences, your perspectives will grow and mature. You may add new items and delete or consolidate others. While it would be unusual to completely reverse any item, it's not out of the realm of possibility. In any of these scenarios, the most important thing is to reflect on why the shift is occurring.

In 2020, when I first shared my Things That Matter at a town hall meeting, I only had eight items. Over the next few years of mentoring and coaching others and of learning more through working with my team, partners, and customers, I added the last two of my current ten, which are Continuous Improvement and Curiosity. These were always important to me, but through learning and experience, I realized it was time to add them to my list and start talking about them as well.

My last two TTM also become the mechanism that helps me to continue to inspect and refine my entire list of TTM. If you seek Continuous Improvement in all things in your professional and personal life, and if you are always Curious, then your TTM will always be a journey and not a destination. As circumstances change in your career or personal life, or you just change your outlook on life, you can and will continue to curate your TTM.

What will also change are the proof points. In all likelihood, you will gain more and more supporting experiences as you strive to live into your Things That Matter. You may also see them exhibited in others more frequently. While this is a form of confirmation bias, it can also be a powerful force for good, especially if your Things That Matter are reflected in real behaviors and are having positive impacts on those around you.

Maintaining your Things That Matter will keep them relevant and current. Maintaining is an action that takes place here and now. Sustaining, in contrast, is an action that projects into the future. When it comes to sustaining your Things That Matter, the focus shifts from updating the list to ensuring you live up to them consistently over time. If you say you believe in Ownership, then you communicate that to others and then follow-up by demonstrating that value in your behaviors, if that becomes visible to people you interact with, well, you can be said to be sustaining your Things That Matter.

Think about your Things That Matter as a promise you make to yourself and others. You are essentially saying, "These are principles that you can count on me following. Moreover, you can count on my adhering to these in a predictable and consistent manner." If you should break that promise, or default on that commitment, you will be letting others down. If they are family members, they may be disillusioned or disappointed; if they are customers or clients, they may not be for long, especially if you're impacting their bottom line.

Every year, every month, every day I gain experiences that continue to shape who I am. That's the way of life. The thing is, unless I pay attention, these lessons will be lost to time. Maintaining and sustaining your Things That Matter is deeply related to Continuous Improvement (TTM #9).

And so, we find ourselves back with Socrates, who, at his trial, is attributed as saying, "An unexamined life is a life not worth living." We have to be present in our own lives; we have to be aware of the commitments we have made and strive to live into them. It takes vulnerability but we should also make corrections along the way when needed. In this way, your Things That Matter can become a self-fulfilling prophecy, a virtuous cycle.

Sources of Inspiration

As you develop your initial list, you may find yourself at a loss as to where to look for the concepts themselves. What source material is appropriate to use in determining your personal list of Things That Matter?

There are two clichés I have often heard in life that I have found to be actually true in almost all cases. One is the golden rule—do unto others as you would have done unto you. It's hard to find an instance where that advice isn't good. The other is, Charity begins in the home. When considering your Things That Matter, start with your own experiences.

In Chapter 1, I shared details about my past that have truly been formative. Experiences that shaped me into who I am today in an undeniable, irrefutable way. For me, this started in my childhood and progressed into my young adult life and early career. Truth be told, it has yet to stop.

In casting back into your previous years, it is helpful to write out your experiences. Journals, memoirs, narratives are all excellent ways to recall and document your past. As you go through this process, you will unlock memories you may have forgotten. Writing about your past can be cathartic.

If you're not prone to writing, the spoken word can also have the same effect. You can record your words in private, or you can record a conversation you have with a trusted friend, colleague, or family member. This technique has the added bonus of having a live feedback mechanism in the form of another person. I have retold events amongst friends and family only to have them cheerily join in and add to the telling, causing me to recall even more detail or correcting details I may have gotten wrong or misunderstood.

Reminiscing about the past isn't an activity reserved for grandparents and old timers. Anyone at any age can retell their histories and past events. In fact, it is a favorite pastime of holidays! An important fact to keep in mind is that some of the most important lessons we learn in life come from negative experiences and even the mistakes we have made. We shouldn't shy away from the more challenging aspects of our past. Often, the most difficult terrain is the most fertile terrain.

I should also note that not all of your Things That Matter need to stem directly from you. They may come from people who were close to you, role models, if you will. I have found that having role models in your life are essential to growth and success. A parent, a sibling, a friend, or a coworker can be role models. You may have seen a certain behavior exemplified by others that you have taken on for yourself. Maybe they were mantras or truths you heard others say that you then saw unfold in your own life, whether at work or at home. For me, my father was also fond of saying, "Charity begins at home." As a child, it was only so many words, but later in my life I saw those words play out so many times in so many ways that they became intrinsic to my thinking and behavior.

When I think of my Things That Matter, I can attribute several to the influence of family, friends, and colleagues. This is not to say that I did not already believe in these values or that I tried to emulate them when I did not personally hold them to be true, rather they were things I knew that mattered to me and when I saw them reflected in the world around me by people I respected…well, that made them all the more valuable.

As noted earlier, one of my leaders, mentors, and friends, George O'Meara, used to say, "Lon, catch people doing the right thing." I still do that today, and this approach led me to my Acknowledge Contributions (TTM #5)—that is, take the time to find and recognize and reward others for doing great things. Don't just look for people doing the wrong things.

Also, my wife Pamela has been a great positive influence on me and has made me a better person and a better leader. Pamela took some of the sharp edge off my approach in dealing with others, causing me to stop and realize that at times I was too harsh in my desire to achieve results. She was able to add some polish to my need to drive results and encouraged me to be a more caring and understanding leader. Pamela's influence led me to focus on Employee First (TTM #6)!

My father, George Essex, influenced me at a very early age to take Ownership and responsibility, which is third on my list of Things That Matter. He demonstrated this every day by being a patriotic American who fought for our country, by being a local community and business leader focused on helping others, and by raising five children after my mother was tragically taken from us when I was only four.

Personally, I think it would be rare to have a list of Things That Matter in which every item was isolated to the person who curated the list. If we see good in ourselves, chances are we picked that up from our environment and from others. They don't just arise in us organically out of thin air. Someone or something helps to place them there.

Another rich source of material is history. As a history nerd and a genealogy buff, this is familiar ground for me, but most people will be cognizant of historical figures and larger-than-life role models. I have a special spot for US presidents who made significant impacts at the global level, individuals who took their convictions and played them out at a large scale to the benefit of entire countries and perhaps even the world. I know people who have been moved by writers and literary figures. There are also athletes, religious figures, military leaders. The list of possibilities is practically endless.

I had the privilege of working close to President Ronald Reagan. While I know people have different views than his and his work as president, I can attest to the power of his character. I will always value my experience seeing that man in action!

President Ronald Reagan was a great leader and known widely as "The Great Communicator." I saw this in action every day in public where he literally changed the world through Effective Communication and Ownership. Behind the scenes at Reagan's ranch, he was down to earth and even humble. He would spend time doing things like riding his horses or chopping wood—just being a cowboy on a western ranch.

Privately he was more like a regular person, and publicly he used his skills and talents to lead the charge against communism and to promote a strong defense posture ("Peace Through Strength").

I remember one time in 1987 at the United Nations (UN); President Reagan was about to go on stage and speak to the UN General Assembly. I was behind the stage in a holding room where the president would wait and collect his thoughts and prepare notes, but in this instance instead of preparing for the speech, Reagan was reading letters from children from around the country and writing personal hand-written responses to them with positive and motivational messages. Then he approached the stage and, as usual, gave a powerful speech that was watched around the world.

I would say that in considering tapping into historically influential people, in using them as possible examples of some of our Things That Matter, the real test is whether they had a lasting impact in a substantive way on our belief system, and more importantly, our observable behaviors. Have we absorbed and ingrained those ideas and values? Have they truly become part of our Things That Matter?

As noted earlier, in adopting Things That Matter from non-internal sources—that is, from sources that don't stem from our own direct experiences, I would caution mimicking values that aren't actually aligned with our own. This is a quick drive to uncomfortable cognitive dissonance at best and years of therapy at worst. Simply put, we should not pretend to be something we aren't. If a perspective doesn't match your own, we should not blind ourselves by trying to wear those lenses. I have known many people who have wasted years and damaged important relationships by earnestly trying to take on beliefs or values that were actually counter to their own.

There is much talk about authenticity, but being authentic is not only an outward projection; it is an internal reflection as well. In fact, authenticity is achieved when what you are on the inside matches what you are on the outside, in both words and actions. I like to think of authenticity as how we behave when we aren't thinking about how we behave. Most people, for instance, will say they are law-abiding citizens with excellent driving habits when in fact they happily and routinely break the speed limit if they aren't being monitored—especially when they have a reason that they believe supersedes the law. Again, I harken back to history—"Know thyself."

Summary

Everyone has Things That Matter. Most people, however, haven't taken the time to truly examine them, much less document them. You don't have to major in Greek philosophy to understand that doing so can be an enriching experience. Becoming clear about the Things That Matter in our lives will not only spur personal growth but will also provide an opportunity to make a difference for those around us, especially if we are leaders.

As you craft your Things That Matter, they will be most meaningful and powerful if they come from your own personal experiences. It is okay to borrow from others but be sure they fit. In considering the sources of our Things That Matter, you should also keep in mind that some of the most powerful lessons we can have will stem from adverse situations. In the end, it isn't the situation that matters so much as what we do with it. A critical aspect of leadership: the indispensable role of Effective Communication in realizing strategic potential. Even the most brilliant strategies and meticulously crafted plans are rendered ineffective if they cannot be clearly and compellingly conveyed to the team responsible for their execution.

"This book is more than advice—it's a compass for anyone who wants to lead with integrity, courage, and purpose in every aspect of life. Authentic, insightful, and deeply personal, Things That Matter reminds us that leadership is not a destination but an adventure—and one that's always worth taking because it's the glue, and if you 'take away the glue and it all falls apart.'"

Patricia Gonzalez, CEO, Real Talk Coaching and Consulting Services

Chapter 5: Communicating Our Things That Matter

The Root of it All

Effective Communication is the very first item on my Things That Matter. It is foundational. It is also tightly interwoven with my other Things That Matter. Effective Communication, in a sense, is the glue of Things That Matter. It holds it all together. Take away the glue, and it all falls apart. Without the adhesive, we are left with a pile of good intentions. When it goes right, when it all sticks together and adheres, we can achieve incredible feats for ourselves, our teams, our customers, and the wider community.

For centuries, people have misquoted the Bible as saying, "Money is the root of all evil" when, in fact, the more accurate quote is "The love of money is the root of all evil." While I'm not qualified to resolve such theological or ethical questions, I can say that *poor communication* is the root of most customer-related problems in businesses today.

Practically all the escalations that come to me on a daily basis have a common root cause of poor communication. By 'escalations,' I mean situations that could not be handled at a lower level but had to be moved upward to a higher level of management for resolution. Thinking over the last ten years, I can recall only one escalation that wasn't related to communication. It had to do with a natural disaster. Although the results of poor communication can feel like a natural disaster, trust me, it is all about human nature. As such, it can be avoided with forethought and practice.

While I see poor communication as a recurrent theme in businesses, it isn't limited to the corporate world. Poor communication cuts across all aspects of life. It's as local as family and friends and as global as politics and economics. It plays out between global leaders and in boardrooms as well as across cubicles and throughout the home.

I've noticed poor communication always seems like the other person's problem. How many times have we thrown our hands up in frustration and exclaimed, "I'm not a mind reader!" The accusation being the other person is to blame for not communicating their expectations clearly. The typical retort is, "I did tell you, but you didn't listen!" The counteraccusation is that the expectations were indeed shared, but the recipient failed to pay attention.

This type of miscommunication happens most often in two-dimensional communications such as texts, online chats, or emails (as opposed to in-person three-dimensional). You can't be an effective communicator if you don't listen. We all need to practice both Effective Communication and Listening. Even with these two skills in motion, there is still room for gaps, unfortunately. Think of the last argument or debate you had in the workplace or even at home with your children or spouse. Chances are it originated from something minor.

In my experience, misunderstandings tend to start small and then grow in severity very quickly, like an avalanche that begins with a small vibration only to become a devastating force of destruction. It's amazing how things as simple as differing points of view, external or internal distractions, or even moods can lead to major disruptions.

Recently, I was driving with my wife to an appointment. My wife pointed to a parking space that I had already prepared to enter. She was attempting to be helpful in case I didn't see the space. I took it as if she were advising me to do something that I was already attempting to do. It was a very simple misunderstanding over an innocent gesture.

Thankfully, we resolved it quickly before it ruined our day and future interactions.

Despite our best intentions, these scenarios happen. We've all been there. Neither party wants to admit to being the source of the misunderstanding. It's natural to believe that we are right and that the other person is wrong. The truth is, however, both parties are right since communication is inherently a two-way process. But the other truth, the more important truth is: just because you're right, doesn't mean you win.

Just Because You're Right, Doesn't Mean You Win

Rarely is there any point to arguing. Ground zero is: I think I'm right; they think they're right. It doesn't mean either of us wins. To get beyond this deadlock, we have to objectively remove ourselves and look at the situation. For most people, this is very difficult to do. It is simply easier to continue with righteous indignation. If we are honest, that burning sense of being right feels good. So good, in fact, it can become addictive to some. Witness the constant flaming and piling on across social media.

I have seen otherwise brilliant salespeople with advanced degrees in business and finance lose an opportunity because of what looks like a price issue on the exterior but it is actually a pride issue on the interior. For instance, in large business deals, $5k can be a rounding error on the accounting sheet, but for the people sitting across the table from one another negotiating the deal, it can be an insurmountable obstacle. A 5K hurdle in a million-dollar project shouldn't be that hard to get over, but I've seen people stand on ceremony and turn their backs on months of hard work. They think: *"I can't lose. I don't want to give in. I don't want to admit defeat and look weak."*

In many business deals, especially sales, there's typically a concern that if a lower price is given, it will set a new bar and establish a bad precedent. If a price break is offered once, it may be expected every time thereafter. A onetime $5k rounding error may become a $500k crisis if replicated over time. The key to avoiding this is to communicate expectations clearly. Is this a onetime deal based on extenuating circumstances, or is this a new pricing baseline to be used in perpetuity?

"Getting to yes" is an Effective Communication strategy that means everyone wins something and usually everyone involved has to compromise some on price, profit, schedule, deliverables, and, yes, on pride. This approach to negotiation emphasizes **principled negotiation**, a method designed to achieve mutually satisfactory agreements by focusing on interests rather than positions, separating the people from the problem, inventing options for mutual gain, and insisting on using objective criteria. There are ways of giving in to demands without setting a dangerous precedent. For instance, one party may be willing to make a concession in order to gain consensus and move things forward. As they do so, they can communicate that repeating the same concession may not work in the future and that it must be respected.

In these scenarios, it comes down to who is at the table and the all-important question of trust. When trust exists, you can have these types of negotiations between people, companies, and even countries! If neither party can trust one another, a $5K gap on a million-dollar opportunity may be the most important thing in the world. Here is the key. In negotiations, you have to "get to yes." Improv troupes teach a variation of this all the time. They say, "yes, and" instead of "yes, but." The point being that "Yes, but" is really just "no" a little prettied up.

The goal should be, "How do we get to yes?" and how can we make sure everybody feels like they've won. If $5K can't be conceded, maybe there are compensatory actions that can be taken. In many transactions and negotiations, there are things that have the quality of "distinction without a difference," meaning giving up something that doesn't have material consequence to one party but does to the other. In this scenario, what can be done that has the weight of $5K that can compensate for the price differential? The answer to this is likely to get both parties to yes. With Effective Communication, both parties can win.

Taking an "I'm right" stance typically results in "you lose"—especially keeping in mind that if the goal is to get everyone to yes, to get everyone to win, then one person losing means everyone loses. In game theory, this is called "zero-sum gain," when the overall sum of the transaction never changes, only the give and take of the parties involved—that is, one person loses exactly what the other person gains. In my experience, people can be so principled that they end up hurting themselves. I'm right; you're wrong. That's it. Now what?

Many years ago, I had the opportunity to lead the sales pursuit and negotiation for a global services engagement with a large financial customer. This was a single trade agreement worth well over $100M. It included negotiating general terms, conditions, pricing, and inclusions at a corporate headquarters (HQ) level and then breaking up into five distinct regions plus dozens of affiliate subsidiaries. As can be imagined, a single deal negotiated at HQ broken into five distinct pieces might not sit well with each of the five global regions. Not surprisingly, each region wanted to then further negotiate an even better deal on their own beyond what was already done at the HQ. I spent well over a full year selling and negotiating between what became six different entities to get everyone to yes.

Throughout the entire process, I used Effective Communication, Listening, Ownership and, maybe most importantly, Transparency to get everyone to sign one single trade agreement with five other co-signers or participants. All parties had to trust me personally and the global trade agreement as well, which took every skill I knew. I was able to gain their trust by representing their desires and needs and by ensuring that everyone saw the value and the benefits.

To summarize, when it comes to Effective Communication, the starting position should be, "How do we get to yes for everyone?" We can't get to yes if we only understand our needs and our goals to the exclusion of others. That's a one-way street to failure. It's the fast lane as well. Getting to yes, getting to real two-way, Effective Communication means knowing your audience as well as you know yourself.

Know Your Audience

As discussed earlier, in discovering our Things That Matter, the most important aspect revolves around knowing ourselves. Earlier I quoted the Greek philosopher, Socrates, as saying, "Know thyself," in relation to discovering our Things That Matter. When it comes to communicating our Things That Matter, our strategy should be to "Know thy audience." Understanding one's audience serves several purposes. As a leader, it can help us understand our team's needs and priorities. This in turn can enable us to collaborate with the team more effectively. In customer-facing roles, understanding one's customers is mission critical. But just how do we get to know our audience?

Understanding your audience is a cornerstone of effective communication, whether you're leading a team, engaging with customers, or crafting public messages. The process involves a multifaceted approach, combining research, observation, and direct interaction to build a comprehensive profile of those you aim to reach. **Key strategies include analyzing past interactions and feedback, utilizing surveys and interviews, and analytics.**

Earlier we covered performance evaluations as a mechanism to know thyself. In getting to know our audience, survey tools and feedback mechanisms can be used similarly. I often use surveys, especially internal surveys, to gather facts and details that help make better decisions, but I also look for the nuances and the sentiments, which usually require reading the detailed notes.

I recently conducted an internal survey to get input from our team of functional leaders to help set strategic priorities and to gather ideas on Continuous Improvement. In the past, I've used targeted surveys with channel partners to look at channel marketing program design features, benefits, and changes. I always take the survey feedback and net it out both in terms of quantitative data and overall sentiment and themes. This data becomes actionable to drive change and Continuous Improvement.

From my experience, surveys can be quite useful when designed well and balanced with other tools. Just like investments and culture, there is strength in diversity. When considering other tools, I group them into two general categories. Ones that cost money and ones that are relatively inexpensive, costing only time and effort.

On the costly side, there are analytics. Most online communication channels can be mined for valuable insights. Whether it's internal corporate announcements, social media, the internet, and intranet websites, there are systems that can extract incredibly rich data. For instance, how many employees actually opened the latest email the CEO sent? Of those who opened the email, how many engaged with it by clicking on an embedded link or opening an attachment? Conversely, how many deleted it immediately? Beyond simple open and click rates, there are sentiment analytics that can determine how people feel about certain topics by studying the words they use in their communications. With recent advancements in AI, we truly are just tapping into this area.

On the less costly side of the equation, we have numerous tools that can yield rich insights and only cost time and effort. One such tool that I've used on multiple occasions with customers and my own teams is the Stop, Start, Continue exercise. The beauty of this exercise is that it can focus on one particular topic, or it can be expanded to address a wide range of topics.

I started using Stop, Start, Continue more than twenty years ago, and it remains a tool I use today. Not only does it yield great actionable results, but it also affords deep insight into how the participants truly feel. As an additional benefit, it can open up great opportunities to personally interact with teams and customers, to get to know them on a human level. Because of this, it is best to conduct this exercise in person.

In the exercise, some general discussion is usually held beforehand to make sure all participants have a baseline understanding of the topic. For instance, if the purpose is to improve a company's performance management program, it would be good to first spend some time reviewing the process. This need not be a lengthy discussion, but enough to refresh the participants on the topic.

Once everyone is up to speed, the first question can be asked. *What should we **stop** doing in our performance management program?* Depending on the number of participants, this can be done in small groups or as one large group. Participants should have time to deliberate over their responses, document them, and then explain them to the other participants. This will initiate rich discussion. Here, an experienced facilitator can help steer the discussion, asking probing follow-up questions to draw out clarifications and delve deeper as needed. The facilitator can also cut off unproductive tangents and help the room stay on track. As a tip, make sure plenty of sticky pads and flip charts are on hand to help capture notes and consolidate themes.

Once the responses for the first questions have been shared and explored, the next question should be asked: *what should we **start or even restart** doing in our performance management program?* The trap to avoid here is to simply state the Stop actions in reverse—e.g., "We should stop making mid-year reviews mandatory" can easily be restated as "We should start making mid-year reviews optional." Again, an experienced facilitator can help with these issues. Similar to the first question, the responses should be documented and explained, allowing ample time for discussion.

The final question is modeled the same way as the others. In our performance management example, it would be: *what should we **continue** doing in our performance management program?* Here the participants discuss current processes that should remain intact. Rarely does a program need to be completely dismantled. Even with the worst programs, there are usually good practices that should be held onto.

I have used this exercise for specific customers, target markets, and new potential markets. It has become a routine tool in my kit that works well every time. I have even used it internally to develop a set of strategic goals and then externally with partners to gather their feedback as well. Each time this creates an opportunity to learn and to ensure the input from others is heard.

The Stop, Start, Continue exercise is a great way to improve processes, practices, services, and even products. It allows the user to gain unfiltered insights into how the participants think about a particular topic, from general disposition to specific details. An important thing to note is that these insights don't just come through the responses and the ideas that are surfaced, but rather through the human interaction of conducting the exercise itself. And to realize that benefit, you have to Listen.

Listening is more than just hearing. One must listen to the comments, the conversations, the discussions—and not only during the formal meeting but during breaks and over meals and especially in the all-important "meeting after the meeting." If you don't listen, you might as well not show up. Few things are worse than asking a question and then walking away before an answer can be given.

In addition to Listening, the other essential aspect of the Stop, Start, Continue exercise is to follow-up on the results. Let me state again that nothing speaks louder than actions. When a leader listens to feedback and then does nothing with that feedback, it sends a very clear message that the leader simply doesn't care.

More than once, I've seen senior leaders attend town halls or sit in on an employee feedback session, get asked some hard questions, make promises, and then fail to follow through with them. This is disappointing and often leads to employees losing trust in that leader or just feeling like they weren't heard, or worse, feeling purposely ignored.

The best way to prevent this is to capture all the feedback, even if there isn't an apparent or immediate answer. Follow up with all participants and share the combined feedback along with common themes, initial priorities and, ideally, some estimated timelines for the priorities. It is as important to call out what CAN'T be acted on as it is to indicate what CAN and what will be done. Being transparent that something cannot be achieved based on other priorities, budget, or timing is a brave act of honesty that most employees will appreciate. In this case, the message becomes: *We heard you. We value your input. This is potentially a great idea, but we can't do it for the following reasons.*

An important side note is that the leader doesn't have to create all the ideas. The leader should inspire others to create and provide ideas. They should then inspire the team to follow through and adopt what is possible while explaining what isn't.

When my previous company merged into my current company, I was holding town halls with employees from both companies. Many had questions about performance bonuses as well as short- and long-term incentives. I responded, "We don't have our systems integrated yet to get visibility into performance that funds and provides these things, but I assure you we'll run the business well, make great choices for our customers, and be transparent when we have visibility about what the results look like."

We ran our region for six months with limited performance visibility and, in the end, we were selected as the Top Region in the World for the entire newly formed company and were able to reward those that contributed to the success. It worked! Meaning we Listened, were Transparent, and used Effective Communication to drive to success even without visibility at the time.

Being Present, Participating, and Playing Back

If you want to get to know your audience—be they customers, partners, employees, friends, or family—you have to talk to them. When leaders ask me for advice on how they should communicate with their teams, how they should really get to know them, they are surprised when my first answer isn't "Hold a town hall meeting" or "Start a social media channel." My answer lacks the sophistication of innovative technology; in fact, it is as old-school as old-school gets. My answer is: *Get out there and talk to them…in person.*

One of my favorite things to do is "walk to the floor." Walking the floor doesn't have to mean literally walking up and down rows of cubicles and stopping to meet with employees. It can be that; doing that is very useful. But it can also be mingling with an audience before an event; it could be having discussions in hallways, elevators, and parking lots. For me, the less formal, the better. It's about meeting people where they are and not standing on formalities. It is more about being approachable and welcoming to all and creating an environment where employees want to approach leadership and have a conversation.

In the military, we used to say, "at ease." Imagine a setting so rigid that you have to literally tell people when to relax because they were so used to being at the ready. Welcome to the military. But surprise! Regular employees in businesses worldwide are like that as well. Just watch how employees stiffen up when the CEO or a senior VP walks into the room. Everyone is on their best behavior and watching their every word and action. You can rest assured that in these circumstances, an employee is unlikely to truly express how they feel about any given matter. They are too afraid of the consequences, of what might happen if their point of view is out of line with the accepted corporate norm. Some people see this as toxic, but it is actually just an exaggerated social norm. It's simply fitting in, or "reading the room."

Regardless of what we call it, I look for ways to make people feel at ease without someone having to actually bark out the command "at ease." For me, this can most effectively be done by being present, participating in the conversation, framing up what you have heard or playing it back, and asking follow-up questions. I know that's a lot, so let's break this down.

Be present. In today's world, it's easier than ever to NOT be present. One of the scariest things to witness today is an entire venue, say a movie theater or restaurant, filled with people who aren't there. I'm not talking about a crazy zombie apocalypse, but rather real living people being completely absent from the moment by obsessing over their phones, by being so absorbed by their own internal dialogue they miss the actual dialogue happening in front of them. We have all seen this. We have all done this.

Being present means breaking the preoccupation and being fully in the moment with the person you are with or, if alone, engaging in one's environment. If that last part seems unusual, think about a time when you arrived at home or at the office without remembering actually traveling there. We joke, "It was like my car was on autopilot." So be present. Put the phone down, pay attention to the person or road in front of you. The best way to be present, by the way, is to participate.

To participate means to meaningfully engage in the interaction at hand. Here we listen to a statement, we absorb it, we respond to it. Sequence is also important. We shouldn't prepare our response when the other person is speaking, but rather after we have listened to their comments, their ideas. A great way to demonstrate you have listened to the other person is by framing up what you have heard. Earlier I characterized this as "netting it out." A word-by-word recitation is not needed. In fact, that would be highly unusual, but a quick summary recapping what one has heard—that is ideal. Not only does it demonstrate good listening habits, but playing something back helps the other person hear how their words or sentiments came across to others. It also gives them an opportunity to clarify or correct if needed.

I had a recent video call with a partner to my company that sells software. I was meeting with all the top leaders, including their chairman. We ran the usual introductions and brief backgrounds to break the ice. The company leaders then proceeded to explain their software products, their desire to grow, and some changes they had made over the years.

When there was a pause, I played their comments back, simply stating, "Let me play back what I heard so we can get agreement on that and then shift to what to do going forward." I then played back in simple terms what I heard. Some of it was nuanced, as in, "I want something from you," so I netted it out by saying, "It sounds like you could use our help in these areas…" They all nodded and agreed.

From there, we had common ground in the past and at least the makings of the future. I listened more and then I typed in the chat feature my recommendations for success going forward. Then we briefly discussed my recommendations and agreed on the paths and actions forward.

Instead of talking past each other for a long period of time, I respected our limited time by netting out, framing up, playing back. With common ground established, we could more easily agree on paths and actions forward, both arriving at yes. It took all of thirty minutes. Done, next!

Clarifying Questions

Another aspect of Listening and getting to know your audience involves asking clarifying questions. For many people, this is a bit painful because they're anxious to get to their idea or express their thoughts, but taking that extra beat to ensure clarity can make all the difference. If during playback, the other person indicates you got it, maybe a clarifying question isn't needed, but from my experience it's usually still appreciated. With follow-up questions, we simply delve more into specifics or possible scenarios. Many times, follow-up questions can lead to fascinating discussions. For instance, if someone tells you at length about a vehicle they want to buy, the follow-up exchange may go as follows:

"So, you're looking to buy a car that's fast but still affordable," you say as your recap.

"That's right. I have a budget, but I still have style!" the other person affirms.

"I know what you mean. I wonder, if you had to choose, would you go with fast but not stylish or stylish but not fast?"

The next response will reveal something about the person's priorities. It may also lead to a great story.

Speak Your Truth

When it comes to communicating your Things That Matter, knowing your audience is as important as knowing yourself. To get to know your audience, you can tap into any number of tools and practices, from surveys to digital analytics to just plain human interaction. I prefer and recommend human interaction both through formal means, such as Stop, Start, Continue exercises, and through informal personal conversations. The key to all these activities is Listening.

Once you know yourself and once you know your audience, the next phase is to speak your truth. A lot has been said in recent years about authenticity. To be effective communicators, we must be authentic. I won't argue with that. I agree wholeheartedly, but let's take a moment to dig into what authenticity actually means.

Authenticity is a powerful approach to interaction that emphasizes honesty, transparency, and genuine self-expression. It involves aligning one's words and actions with their true thoughts, feelings, and values, fostering deeper connections and building trust.

Being authentic is more than spouting empirical truths that we believe because they are actual facts. For instance, saying that we believe the sun will rise tomorrow may be a statement of fact, but it doesn't convey authenticity. For one, we have no stake in the game. The sun will rise tomorrow regardless of any action we take. Saying we believe in acknowledging the contributions of others and then actually doing it—that's authenticity. We say it and we demonstrate it.

I've had the privilege of working for some great and authentic leaders who influenced me and helped shape my Things That Matter. An interesting thing about authenticity is that it has a tremendous halo effect. For instance, when we work for authentic leaders, it tends to advance our own brand. The organization sees that we report to an authentic leader, and they are more likely to trust us from the start or at least give us the benefit of the doubt. It "raises your stock," so to speak, just by being associated with an authentic leader.

One of my first leaders during my time at the White House was another US Air Force member, Gary Lau. Gary and I went on to work together at other companies as partners and teammates and had many years of success working together. Gary was honest, trustworthy, ethical, respectful, and more. Everyone knew that. He was the leader whom others trusted to deliver on his commitments even in times of stress and pressure, which every leader will face. Not once across multiple decades that I worked with him did I ever witness him breach his integrity. Gary was a leader who had customers stay with him for many years because they trusted his words and his actions. He was an influencer before that was a thing. I learned a lot from Gary, and I still demonstrate those traits today.

The two factors that increase the value of authenticity are reliability and consistency. Reliability speaks to how well others can depend on us to behave in a certain way over time. This isn't only a human quality; customers expect businesses to be reliable as well. For instance, if an internet company undergoes frequent outages, it won't take long for their customers to find new providers. The customer expects reliable service.

Consistency, on the other hand, indicates how well we live up to a certain standard. For example, if an internet service provider has no outages but delivers intermittent levels of bandwidth—sometimes high and sometimes low—customers are likely to go in search of a new provider. It isn't enough that the company is providing a service; that service has to be consistently good.

Authenticity operates the same way for people as it does for companies. If a leader says they acknowledge the contributions of others but only rarely does so, employees will see them as inauthentic based on a lack of reliability. In addition, if the leader's acknowledgements for similar contributions are sometimes insignificant (a nod in the hallway) and at other times extravagant (cash rewards given out at employee galas), the leader will again be viewed as inauthentic, this time due to inconsistent standards.

When it comes to Things That Matter, we should place nothing on our lists that we do not authentically believe or which we are unwilling to live into on a reliable and consistent basis. We must speak our truth, and we must live that truth. Espousing a belief and then acting counter to that belief only creates mistrust. A leader who cannot be trusted is not a leader at all.

Stand and Deliver

I've seen enough consummate communicators in action—from President Reagan to John T. Chambers (former CEO of Cisco) to numerous military leaders—to know that there is both an art and a science to communications. **Communication is considered both an art and a science due to its dual nature: it involves systematic principles and observable phenomena (science), alongside the creative and intuitive application of those principles in human interactions (art).** Good speakers and good writers don't happen by accident. They deliberately hone their skills—they study, practice, learn from coaches and trainers alike. Now, I'm not saying that an advanced communication degree is required to communicate one's Things That Matter. However, being able to speak well, write well, and show up well will lend a degree of credibility, or ethos as our friend Socrates might say, to one's Things That Matter.

In the business world, there are ample opportunities to develop strong presentation skills. Every leader should take media training, including refreshers every few years. Media training includes intensive drilling on communicating under stressful situations such as broadcast interviews and executive presentations. It usually includes the fundamentals of communications—defining your purpose and message; understanding the audience; and, of course, delivering with confidence and credibility. Improv tactics are usually taught as well as tips on how to dress, stand, move, and even sit while communicating. Media training typically takes several days, but the skills learned will last a lifetime—or at least until the next refresher!

From my experience, the best approach to improve one's communication is through a professional communication coach who can work with you on a one-to-one basis, critiquing your skills and helping to strengthen weaknesses and enhance strengths. Most importantly, they provide an objective perspective and can give constructive feedback where others may be inhibited from doing so. The Emperor's New Clothes, though taught as a childhood fable, is a very real modern phenomenon. Don't expect your employees to always provide you with sensitive feedback. They may see it as too risky or simply impolite or undiplomatic. For this, a trusted advisor is needed.

The good news is that there are ample development programs, media training courses, and communication coaches in the market. Several years ago, I attended a seminar for executives where we had to stand and present on any topic with no warning for about five minutes. We were mostly graded and measured on our style and not the content. Every presentation was recorded and played back to the entire class with plenty of commentary from the coach and even the peer group. To be clear, this was two kinds of pressure. One, the simple act of being recorded without pauses or retakes to adjust. Second, receiving unfiltered feedback not only from a coach but from peers. Both of these scenarios can be nerve-wracking.

Now, before that program, I had been doing public speaking for years and had always enjoyed it. I had been through various internal and external courses to learn more. In this case, this very immersive and highly critical bootcamp was far more intense than any other media training I had ever done. I am unsure if there is a cause-and-effect relationship there, but there is certainly correlation. Overall, the experience proved to be very valuable. Since then, many people have complimented me on my public speaking. When they do, I always thank them and then add, "I trained for this." And boy, did I!

While speaking skills are perhaps best learned through training, executive presence is best improved with the help of a coach. Executive presence, in a sense, is how we show up. It includes posture, body language, gestures, eye contact—a multitude of nonverbal clues that project confidence and composure. It also includes how one dresses and behaves. Do we show up on time for meetings? Are we prepared? Are we relaxed? Do we help others to feel relaxed? Executive presence requires equal measures of self-awareness and empathy, or emotional intelligence. There are also plenty of books and online resources available, though the most important factor is being able to access unfiltered, objective feedback.

Writing with Style

I have left the topic of writing skills for last. Writing skills are what I like to call longwave skills—that is, they take time and patience to develop. The key tactics are study and practice, two things that anyone can do…also, two things that most people hate doing. My advice: bite the bullet and just do it.

A few tips to consider. First, studying doesn't need to be painful. You don't have to read the latest edition of Strunk & White's *Elements of Style,* though I do recommend it, or the *AP Style Guide,* also recommended, to improve your writing. Regularly reading good books, journals, and newspapers will also help.

While *Anna Karinina* and *Don Quixote* are indeed masterpieces, writing your next town hall script or email in the style of Tolstoy or Cervantes might be a little offsetting to your intended audience. Which is to say, there's no need to run off to the classics section of your local bookstore to buy a stack of books you'll probably end up never reading. By the same token, it may be wise to indulge less in social media and more in long-form publications. The idea is that when we immerse ourselves in good writing, we pick up good writing habits. Although not quite by osmosis, we tend to absorb good writing practices through consistent exposure. If you are able, of course, it is also recommended to slow down when you read these types of publications and note things like punctuation, grammar, and style. At the same time, much writing is done or at least revised with the help of AI tools. AI tools are useful and helpful but should not be a substitute for solid writing skills if you want to maintain authenticity.

I had a high school English teacher who told me I would never make anything of myself because of my less than eager desire to write. Maybe it was because that teacher told me that I couldn't do something, but I became dead set on improving my writing skills as I started my career. Keep in mind, in those years writing was a much more manual process than it is today. When I joined the military, we still used typewriters. I didn't know how to type at all. Some high schools had mandatory classes in typewriting. Mine didn't. And here I was in a job that required volumes of written and formal communications to higher commands. With no YouTube videos or apps on my phone (those were still science-fiction at the time), I had to learn and practice the old-fashioned way—by just doing it.

Biting the bullet and still hearing that high school teacher's words in my head, I began writing more. I always enjoyed reading, so I also read more. All of my jobs after the military required me to write more in terms of proposals and formal communications. I discovered that the more I applied myself, the better I became. Even in my personal life, I found opportunities to write. Over time, I became the family genealogist, writing small papers such as narratives and histories. I kept doing it until I was a much better writer. In a sense, I was self-taught. Now I help others with writing skills. We are all capable of achieving success in many areas if we focus and put our minds to it.

Beyond self-development, similar to speaking and presentation courses, the market is filled with writing courses. I recommend these as well. A good course can help with the basics of writing, and many provide useful good-for-all-seasons tips.

For those who work in medium- to large-sized companies, a communications team is likely to be available. Use them, but use them wisely. "Unwisely" is giving them free rein to write all your materials; "wisely" is working closely with them to ensure they capture your message and your voice appropriately. Wisely also includes spending time with them to learn how they craft your material so you can learn along the way.

Summary

If your Things That Matter are meaningful to you, you should take care to Effectively Communicate them. Speaking well, showing up well, and writing well will help to ensure your Things That Matter are understood and respected.

Discovering, documenting, and communicating our Things That Matter will get us a long way down the field, but they won't quite get us across the finish line. Words and presence are important; they are a type of promise; however, as we noted with authenticity, if our actions and results fail to fulfill those promises, we will reap nothing but turmoil and mistrust. The final phase we will examine is demonstrating our Things That Matter.

> *"A down-to-earth guide on what real leadership looks like. Essex takes you through his own remarkable journey, from a small-town boy working at his family's grocery store to a successful leader...Each chapter blends real-life stories with practical lessons, showing that leadership isn't about titles or power, it's about service, resilience, and helping others succeed. Leadership is not something you are born with or just for a select few, instead it is built. Whether you're stepping into your first leadership role or looking to refine your approach after years of experience, Things That Matter gives you a practical, honest roadmap. A must read!"*
>
> **Kimberly Escobar, Director, Dynamic Contracting, Inc.**

Chapter 6: Demonstrating Things That Matter

When first developing our Things That Matter, it may be difficult to remember all eight to ten items and what they specifically mean, much less remembering to authentically demonstrate them throughout our daily activities. I recommend simply writing them down for quick and easy reference. I keep mine saved on my phone so I can add notes and reflections as they occur to me. Others may prefer pen and paper. It all comes down to preference and what we're comfortable with. Of course, the more we put them into practice, the more they'll commit to memory and the more natural they'll become.

First step: document and reference your Things That Matter regularly to keep them top of mind.

Second step: do them.

We've all heard it said that "actions speak louder than words." It's a valid statement, one that we've all seen play out either at home or in the workplace. Building on that, writer, poet, activist Maya Angelou is quoted as saying, "I've learned that people will forget what you said, people will forget what you did, but people will never forget how you made them feel." Another valid statement. I especially appreciate that it gets at the *impact* our words and actions have on others.

Through our words and actions, we can make people feel wanted and valued. We can make them feel heard and validated. We can inspire; we can motivate. As leaders, this ability to move people is critical. Another type of impact we can have is to instill trust.

In my experience, trust is created through reliability and consistency. As noted earlier, reliability speaks to how well others can depend on us to behave in a certain way over time. Consistency, on the other hand, indicates how well we live up to a certain standard. If we act one way on Monday and then act in a contradictory way on Tuesday, we have a problem. If we do this regularly, if we create a trend line of erratic behavior, those we interact with will find it hard to forget and even to forgive. This is why authenticity is so important. Authenticity engenders trust.

Sadly, it is becoming more and more difficult to find someone these days who engenders authenticity and trust without controversy. This seems to be a product of hyperpolarization, which we see running rampant almost everywhere. Even some of our influential and recognized leaders who achieved great things are often criticized by popular culture for some element of their lives. Social media has made this phenomenon a lot worse, providing a platform for people to criticize everything and everyone, often based on questionable agendas, mis-informed opinions, or plain malice. Whereas we should be measuring a person's authenticity based on the whole person and not necessarily one small component.

No one is exempt from this sad state of affairs. I have to think back to Pope John Paul II, who passed away in 2005, as an example of someone who was loved by many for being authentic. I worked at the White House when the Cold War was front and center around the world. During this time, I witnessed Pope John Paul II partner with President Ronald Reagan and Prime Minister Margaret Thatcher to end the Cold War and communism in the Eastern Bloc at that time. Together, they walked the talk and worked closely to ensure freedom for millions of people who still benefit from their influence today. They demonstrated the power of authenticity can truly have a tremendous impact for the good.

Another thing I have found to be true about authenticity is that it is almost impossible to fake. This idea seems inherent by definition—that is, you can't fake authenticity—but almost everyone has experienced someone who has tried to do this. People notice it like an uncanny sixth sense. Now, I'm not suggesting it is supernatural. Quite the opposite. I firmly believe that sensing authenticity is rooted more in practical matters. Specifically, authenticity becomes noticeable through how well our behaviors meet the promise of our words.

Taken one step further, when things are authentic to us, we tend to demonstrate them by second nature. This tendency plays out in some interesting and important ways. One is during the interview process, where the interviewer tries to discover through carefully crafted questions if the candidate has the right skills and behaviors needed for a role. Throughout my career, I have conducted hundreds of interviews, and I am often called upon to conduct them in numerous capacities. As such, I'm always on the lookout for new interview techniques. Some time ago, I discovered that my Things That Matter can be a great tool to help determine if a person is suitable for a particular role or a promotion.

Interviewing for Things That Matter

When interviewing candidates for a position, I have in mind key skills and behaviors that I believe are required to be successful in the role. My task in the interview is to see if the interviewee has those skills and behaviors and, if so, at what level. To do this, I ask them to share an experience about one of those competencies. If I'm interviewing for a project manager, for instance, I might ask about Ownership (TTM #3). I see Ownership—a keen sense of accountability, persistent follow-through, a drive for results—as an essential to the role of a project manager. Another of my favorite questions revolves around Curiosity (TTM #10). I like to end interviews with, "Tell me a story about how you used Curiosity to help improve a customer situation or solve a customer problem." The response to this always tells me a great deal about the candidate!

When interviewing, it's important to remember that it's easy for someone to explain the theory of a thing without having any practical experience in actually doing the thing. I like to think about it as the difference between making or changing the news versus simply reporting the news. When building a high-performing team, I want people who make or change the news and who don't just report it. If I want theory, I can turn on any podcast or pick up a textbook. I want people with actual hands-on experience, with a track record of demonstrating the skills I need on the team. More than that, I want people who demonstrate the skills in ways that have a notable impact on the end result.

I've found that if something is important to someone, if it is in their DNA, they'll be able to relate multiple examples of when they demonstrated it. It will be part of their history and who they are. When a person taps into these matters, when they uncover stories in their work history and start telling stories about Things That Matter to them, their eyes light up, they become enthusiastic, and they lean forward—literally and figuratively.

It's hard to admit, but over our careers we will inevitably make bad hiring decisions. It's an easy trap to fall into. First, everyone puts their best self on display during an interview. Second, we tend to hear what we want to hear. Confirmation bias is where individuals tend to seek, interpret, and recall information in a way that confirms or supports their pre-existing beliefs or values. Confirmation bias can be a true obstacle at times. Maybe we just get a good feeling about someone for a particular role only for the disappointing truth to set in later. We might find the candidate was great at reporting the news, which came through during the interview, but not so great at making or changing the news, which comes through in actual workplace performance. In other words, we sometimes find that despite our best hopes, a newly hired employee doesn't perform to standards or have the impact that's required to be successful.

This is most likely to happen when someone we know, who is already on the team or on an allied team, interviews for and then steps into a new role—an internal hire. We may think the person has the right skills based on their performance and impact in a prior role that we had visibility to. Based on that, we let our guard down. In our mind we have already cast them in the new role, and we assume they'll be successful because that's how we saw them in the past. It's always a hard fact to face when we realize we let our assumptions get the best of us.

This could just as easily happen when interviewing external candidates, but since we don't have direct experience with their previous performance, we go by what the candidate reports either in the interview or on their resume. And let's face it, some people can tell great stories, and there is always a part of us that wants that candidate to succeed. Meaning we want to believe in them, and we can sometimes hear more in an answer or read more into a resume than what is actually there.

I have had both scenarios happen more than once in my career, and now I take steps to avoid them. I also teach others to do the same. I recall a situation that happened about fifteen years ago. A very long time, by some people's standards, but the lesson I learned still sticks with me.

We had an internal candidate interview for a promotion and an associated international relocation. This person was a top performer in a sales support role and was widely supported by his peers and teammates. His performance reviews were glowing, and his results undeniable. It seemed like a natural progression for him to take a high-profile role on our sales team. Hindsight shows that even at this early stage in the selection process we were already heavily biased to select him for the role. Why? We wanted him to succeed. We wanted him to succeed because it confirmed our thinking, and it also leaned into the faulty logic that if he succeeded in one role, he would therefore succeed at another although the roles were clearly different.

Needless to say, with this type of momentum, the interview process was quick. It felt like a foregone conclusion, but it also felt like the right conclusion. The previous performance was there, albeit in a different role and with a different function, and they had plenty of allied support. With little fanfare and even less surprise, the person was selected to move to a direct sales role and subsequently an international relocation to the US.

To be clear, this wasn't an ordinary promotion and relocation. Expatriate roles are very pricey for a company. Not only is there an increase in compensation and benefits with cost-of-living differentials and expat premiums weighing in, but there is also endless red tape with work visas and residency requirements. Working abroad can be taxing, in a social and emotional way, for an individual and their family; but it can also be taxing, in a literal way, for the company who sponsors them!

Imagine our disappointment, then, when soon after the individual relocated and settled in it became evident that he didn't actually possess the skills needed to grow into the new role. The ability needed to perform and deliver sizeable sales results plus the attention to detail, follow-up, forecasting, and all the rest associated with being an account manager at a leading networking and technology provider were simply not there. He had great interview skills and had an excellent performance record in a supporting role. He also had deep and wide organizational support, but he did not have the requisite skills to perform well in a senior-level sales role. This was a pricey lesson for the company and a difficult position for the employee.

Since that time, I now follow a more structured team interview process that includes several one-on-one interviews with team members associated with the new team and with a few members who are removed from the team. We start with a set of scoring criteria along with a scale used for all candidates and by all those involved in the interview process. Scoring is tabulated at the end of each round and narrowed down until there are two remaining candidates, who then go to higher-level interviews. The lesson I learned was that to break the many biases that are inherent when managing internal advancements, you have to follow a consistent, broad, and structured process and dig deep to assess the right set of criteria. And because no process is ever perfect, even with these protocols in place, there is still room for errors and gaps.

I have learned that finding the right candidate for a role isn't just about technical skills and expertise. It's also more than having healthy workplace behaviors such as a strong work ethic, a capacity for collaboration, and versatile interpersonal skills. Beyond these key areas, there is also the matter of cultural fit, team dynamics, and how the portfolio of customers and partners will work with the individual. This is where having clarity on Things That Matter can help.

Today, I use several of my Things That Matter to formulate interview questions such as Core TTMs like Effective Communication, Listening, and Ownership as well as Transformational and Aspirational TTMs such as Transparency and Curiosity. These give me a value-centric perspective of the candidate and help me gauge how well they'll fit into the culture I'm striving to establish. This approach is rooted in the principle that a candidate's values and behaviors are strong indicators of their success within a particular organizational environment. Effective Communication, for instance, is a core TTM that assesses a candidate's ability to convey ideas clearly and concisely, and to understand others' perspectives. Listening, another core TTM, evaluates a candidate's capacity to actively comprehend information, which is crucial for collaboration and problem-solving. Ownership, as a core TTM, gauges a candidate's willingness to take responsibility for their actions and outcomes. Transformational TTMs like Transparency emphasize open communication and honesty, fostering trust within the team. Curiosity, an aspirational TTM, highlights a candidate's desire to learn, explore, and innovate, which is vital for growth and adaptability.

Have a Plan

Over the years I have learned that when our Things That Matter are genuine, they'll naturally flow, energizing us and those around us. The trick is to be aware of them, to tap into them at the appropriate time to drive the appropriate results. Now, we can wait around and just hope that these opportunities avail themselves all on their own. Writer Antoine de Saint-Exupéry referenced this type of naivete in his novella, *Le Petite Prince*, or *The Little Prince* in English, when he wrote, "A goal without a plan is just a wish." We can wait around and wish for our Things That Matter to manifest themselves at the right time, or we can help the process along by regularly reviewing our Things That Matter, reflecting on them with unflinching honesty, and looking for opportunities to demonstrate them with authenticity.

I hold to the premise that we should do things "by design, and not by default." This philosophy emphasizes taking intentional control over one's life rather than passively reacting to circumstances. It's about consciously shaping your future, aligning actions with values, and pursuing a purposeful existence. It is how I approach Ownership and it's a guiding light that I follow constantly as I conduct business and as I walk through life. From my perspective, everything should be done with purpose and intent.

Most professionals know the value of preparing for meetings. If we call a meeting, it's important for those attending to know the purpose of the session and to have a sense of the agenda. They will also need to know who is attending and what they're expected to contribute. At the end of the meeting, it's a good idea to circulate minutes, which document key information such as what was discussed, what was agreed, and, most important, what action items were assigned to whom. The minutes of the meeting become the official record of the event. In the business world, this process of planning and documenting meetings is part of business as usual. When it comes to our Things That Matter, a similar practice is needed.

In a sense, our Things That Matter become our purpose and agenda that we should be mindful of throughout the course of our day, week, month. The same way we take notes during a meeting to capture key items for future reference, we should make a practice out of taking time at the end of each day or week to reflect on how we demonstrated our Things That Matter. This can be as formal as a journal or as informal as a mental exercise. The key point is, we need to consciously keep account of our actions, or they'll be lost in the blur of our daily activities.

If Listening is one of our Things That Matter, for instance, we should be able to recall if and when we practiced active listening during the day. Taking time to make some notes about what happened, who was involved and what the results were will help to keep the matter top of mind in the coming days. In this way, reflecting and doing become a cycle.

"Did we demonstrate Listening?"

If yes, how did it go? What went well? What can we improve? If not, how can we identify opportunities to do so?

I recall a virtual group meeting I held. There were eight to ten individuals involved, with me being the most senior member present. For some reason, I found myself trying to race to what I thought were the answers to solving the customers' problems. Maybe in that moment I thought that because I was the senior member, I should have all the answers. Maybe I had other pressing matters I wanted to get to. To be honest, I can't recall exactly what my rush was—but what I do keenly recall is the realization that I had violated one of my Core TTMs, Listening (TTM #2). This wasn't apparent to others, but it was to me. It was a rude wake-up call for me, one that I still remember vividly. In the end, things worked out well with the customer. It also worked out for me, providing me with an important lesson. Again, Mistakes can often be a strong tool for Continuous Improvement (TTM #9).

Today, I use a mental scorecard to keep track of how well I am doing with my Things That Matter during the day and week, and then I course correct dynamically and move forward. Like any sport where we may start with written instructions and notes to guide us, later we develop muscle memory that helps us to inherently know if we are off our game.

Get Action

One of the US presidents I admire most is our twenty-sixth president, Theodore Roosevelt. At forty-two, he was the youngest to take the office, and that still stands today. His accomplishments as a president are many—negotiating the end of the Russo-Japanese War; setting aside US national forests, preserves, parks, and monuments; leading the Panama Canal initiative to completion; strategically strengthening the US Navy. He was also a prolific writer, a rancher, and a devoted husband and father. Truly a man of all seasons.

While all of this is more than noteworthy, what I admire most about President Theodore Roosevelt are his personal traits, the principles he espoused and lived by. His legacy, his history, is one of actionable authenticity; that is, his behaviors matched his words. One such trait was his drive to get things done. To "get action."

Long before Nike was telling us to "just do it," President Roosevelt was encouraging people to "get action." The longer version runs as follows: *Get action. Do things; be sane; don't fritter away your time; create, act, take a place wherever you are and be somebody; get action.*

In this quote, the implicit doer of the action is us. Simply put, we have to take ownership to get action. When it comes to Things That Matter, no one is going to do it for us. We have to get action and make it happen with purpose and intent...by design, and not by default!

When a Mistake Becomes a Virtue

As a word of caution, as we get action, as we follow our plan, things may not always go according to script. Keeping in mind my principle of Predictive Follow-up (TTM #7), we shouldn't be surprised when we falter. While we should seek to minimize these instances, we should also be of the mindset to learn from our mistakes. This is also part of Continuous Improvement (TTM #9). Many of the most lasting lessons we will ever experience will come from our mistakes.

Now, I'm not advocating that we all go out and purposefully make a long series of mistakes in an effort to perfect ourselves. What I am saying is that when we make mistakes, we should be mindful of what went wrong, why it went wrong, and what we can do in the future to avoid it. In doing so, we'll often find a key principle or value residing at the root. In my experience, every good habit has an origin story, and often those origin stories begin with a mistake.

One of my most memorable experiences of a misstep that I was later able to turn into a golden lesson involved Ownership (TTM #3) and Continuous Improvement (TTM #9). I was negotiating a major deal with a mega-company. This company commanded a spend north of a billion dollars per year. As one might imagine, the sheer pressure and weight they could exert was tremendous. I had to be careful, therefore, to have enough checks and balances built into their contract to ensure they couldn't unfairly overpower their smaller competitors and put those firms out of business. The mega-company would love this, and of course it was part of their strategy, if not explicitly then at least implicitly.

When this matter came to the test, I stood up to them. Thinking I was doing the right thing, I essentially said, "I can't agree to these terms because they will create an unfair advantage against other partners." I was willing to believe my sense of ethics would trump their sense of profits.

Not surprisingly, their response was unfavorable, to say the least. I could see plainly that they wanted to be the giant and crush the others. From their perspective, though, they had earned that right, and all was fair in the ultra-competitive world of business. Also, it was their modus operandi, and they were used to getting their way. I felt like I was the valiant hero protecting the line, but in their eyes, I was the annoying obstacle holding up progress.

This is where the lesson comes in. What I failed to do was Seek Assistance (TTM #8). Instead of choosing to face the mega-company alone, I should have gone to someone higher in my organization who could have fortified our position. As it was, I was seen as a bad team player—at best non-cooperative, at worst, too rigid. To fix the problem, they made a few well-placed calls and asked that I be removed from the negotiations. My company readily complied. Believe me, being taken off such a high-level, highly visible project was for a moment a relief. For just one second, I felt all the pressure just lift, but what followed very quickly wasn't so uplifting. The situation was severely humbling and potentially career-limiting if not career-ending. In trying to do the right thing, I almost triggered a critical failure.

Thankfully, while my management agreed to take me off of the project, they also took the time to assess the scenario and made sure I was protected. I came to learn that this was one of those missions where a unit goes behind the lines and somebody's not coming back. That's just how it is sometimes. In business, you have to have a thick skin and learn not to take things personally. Sometimes difficult decisions have to be made. As noted earlier, just because you're right doesn't mean you win. This reminds me of a mentor who taught me "that the right message at the wrong time is the wrong message."

Anyone who has fallen off a proverbial horse will know that one of the possible consequences is becoming risk-averse. Aversion to risk is good if taken in a measured way. This is why the field of enterprise risk management exists. There is a point, though, when an otherwise healthy aversion turns into fear and becomes a detriment to growth. In this way, fear in business, in leadership, in life, is rarely a good thing. At the end of my experience with the bad negotiation, I had a choice to learn from the incident or to be overwhelmed by it. I chose the former, opting to overcome the obstacle to what would become key tenets of my Things That Matter: Ownership (TTM #3) and Continuous Improvement (TTM #9).

One Foot on the Gas and One on the Brake

In the US, most cars come equipped with an automatic transmission. It's different in Europe and other parts of the world where the roads are generally narrower, twisty, and hilly. Manual transmissions give drivers more command of the road and control of the vehicle. Also, at least in my opinion, they're more fun to drive. Many drivers in the US miss out on the pleasure of downshifting to get more torque as they push up a hill or upshifting on an open road as the RPMs top out. On the other hand, automatics are lifesavers in cities like San Francisco!

Growing up in rural East Tennessee, I learned to drive a standard transmission coupled with manual brakes and manual steering. I had to drive all manner of vehicles—from forklifts, tractors, motorcycles, track loaders—if it had wheels or tracks, I could drive or ride it. When I joined the military, I was thankful for those skills and was required to operate other vehicles. But here's the thing: when you're operating a vehicle with more than two pedals plus a stick shift in addition to a dashboard of levers, knobs, and dials, it's easy to lose your rhythm, our sense of balance, and activate the wrong mechanism in the wrong sequence.

When we seek to demonstrate Things That Matter, we need to be conscious of the need for balance. With up to ten principles to tap into and with all the best intentions to demonstrate them, it's easy to lose our balance. Perhaps we lean into one behavior too often and with too much force, causing those around us to question our authenticity or see us as one-dimensional. Alternatively, we may lightly tap on all the behaviors so quickly that it becomes a blur to those we interact with, causing confusion and uncertainty as to what our priorities may be. When practicing our Things That Matter, we need to exercise balance.

As leaders, there are times that we have to push hard to drive initiatives forward and to show progress toward our common goals. However, at times we must also throttle back and briefly pause, only to move forward later and continue onward toward success. Then there are times we must do both; meaning we push hard on some points while being cautious and tentative in order to achieve our common goals without causing harm or damage. This is a delicate balance that leaders need to practice and ideally perfect on a daily basis, and this notion extends well beyond our Things That Matter. Racecar drivers often enter curves at high speed with one foot on the gas and one on the brake, a technique known as "left-foot braking" to allow for forward momentum while reducing some risk of taking the curve too fast.

A compelling business example illustrating the dynamic leadership approach of pushing hard, pausing, and simultaneously pushing and being cautious can be found in the **pharmaceutical industry, specifically during the development and launch of a novel drug.** This sector inherently demands both aggressive pursuit of innovation and meticulous risk management due to the high stakes involved in human health and significant financial investments.

Specifically, I recall when I first joined Cisco, the culture and the acceptable practice typically at the end of every quarter was the "diving catch." The company was filled with scores of quarter-end stories and heroic finishes to drive results. For a time, this was celebrated and in time expected. Then as the company grew this became an unacceptable behavior that was too risky for an industry giant. The culture moved from mostly "the gas" to leveraging the gas and the brake" efficiently.

Having our Things That Matter as a solid foundation to anchor us can help us to lead with confidence and drive our teams forward to achieving common goals with finesse. Sadly, the alternative that I've seen many leaders opt for is to strive to achieve common goals at any cost. In this equation, the "common goals" is a great numerator, but "at any cost" is a terrible denominator. From my experience, leaders tend to invoke the "at any cost" clause as an excuse to push people beyond acceptable limits, to take unwise risks, and to even bend ethical standards at times, none of which are good practices. We should always keep one foot on the gas and one on the brake—not a practice I recommend while driving unless you are a race car driver, but a great way to maintain balance as a leader who is responsible for getting actions while also managing risks!

Encoding Things That Matter

One of the best ways to consistently demonstrate a value is to embed it into the way of working across an organization. This becomes especially powerful when done at an enterprise level across an entire company but can also be impactful when done at a team level.

One of the many things John Chambers, former CEO of Cisco, was known for was the value he placed on communications. He implemented multiple programs at Cisco to build the company's communications muscle. One practice was for executives to receive ratings on their presentation skills, both for delivery and content, whenever they presented at internal or customer-facing events. This was supported by communication development programs. Chambers made it abundantly clear to the employees of Cisco that Effective Communication was a priority to him—and not just because he personally valued good communication, but because he believed it was good for business.

When I worked for Cisco, we used voicemail extensively. Today, voicemail seems like an antiquated technology akin to the fax machine, but in its time, it was quite an innovation. At Cisco in the 1980s through the early 2000s, voicemail was used extensively. We had pre-set distribution lists and forwarding options; we could copy, we could save—pretty much anything you can do with emails today you could do with voicemail then.

Of course, with something used so heavily, there had to be a protocol around its proper use. In Cisco, which again had a deep culture for communications, it was normal to send voicemails to senior leaders only to receive them back graded with specific details around how to improve brevity, specificity, and overall impact.

Importantly, this feedback process wasn't meant to be a form of criticism or to be judgmental; it was meant to refine and polish communications that could and would be forwarded up-channel to C-level leadership and likely be redistributed to even larger audiences. In the framework of Things That Matter, it was Effective Communication meets Continuous Improvement!

Encoding Things That Matter into a day-to-day, regular routine, however, doesn't require a ubiquitous system with rules and guidelines for proper usage. It also doesn't require us to be the CEO of an entire organization. Neither does it have to be done in a formal or unfeeling way. Often, people assume systematic means robotic. It doesn't. Just like we need to have scheduled syncs with our employees and teammates we need to do the same with our family and friends.

My wife and I have something we call "LifeSync." LifeSync is a routine we have on the schedule, both hers and mine. I often say if you want to know what's important to someone, check their calendar. We calendar things that we don't want to forget. Every other Sunday evening, my wife and I have LifeSync when we not only align our schedules, but we also align ourselves with each other, making sure that we have clear communication. While we note things like events and travel, the true root of our exchange are questions like "Do you need help with anything?" or "Is anything driving you crazy?"

To me, our LifeSync routine is about Effective Communication (TTM #1) and Listening (TTM #2). Making time to share information, thoughts, feelings with one another clearly requires communicating, and it also requires that the other person listens. For our LifeSync to work, we have to speak, and we have to listen. We also have to be authentic, and we have to follow through on our commitments. In this way, Ownership (TTM #3) also comes into play. If I say, "I need you to do this," or she says, "We need to do more of that," there has to be some commitment to do those things.

We've been doing LifeSync for many years. When we first started doing it, it was a matter of necessity. With two busy schedules, we had to get a line on where we were both going to be at any given moment or we would end up missing each other, literally and figuratively. We very quickly got past the logistics and tactical aspects and realized we also had to sync up on more important matters. Today, we both believe our habit of LifeSync is an essential component of our marriage. I recommend you apply this to your professional and personal lives!

A compelling business example of "encoding Things That Matter into a day-to-day, regular routine" without requiring a ubiquitous system or formal, unfeeling methods can be observed in Patagonia's commitment to environmental sustainability and ethical sourcing. This isn't a top-down mandate enforced through rigid rules, but rather an ingrained philosophy that permeates their operational DNA, from product design to supply chain management and customer experience. Again, Things That Matter don't have to be limited to the workplace. In fact, I would suggest that if your Things That Matter are genuine and essential to you, they'll spill over into all areas of your life. And this is a good thing.

Don't Outrun the Supply Wagon

Creating a reliable track record of meeting one's commitments is an essential component of building trust in any relationship, be it personal or professional. Even stock markets rely on trust. Investors gain trust in a company when the company reliably meets their forecast. If they come in under the forecast, it's clearly bad. Investors question the leadership's ability to steer the ship. If they are over, it's also bad. In this scenario, it suggests capital may have been left on the table that could have been better allocated. All in all, a business's ability to meet their forecast can make or break their reputation.

Similarly, reliably and consistently doing what we said we were going to do is a critical measure of leadership. They say words are cheap. In the world of social media, this is especially true. What does hold value, though, is the premium of following through on commitments and promises. As leaders, we have to be careful not to outrun the supply wagon and fail to meet the expectations we have set or to get too far ahead of ourselves in regard to what is possible for ourselves or our teams to achieve. This can happen when we over-promise our employees or teams.

Consistently delivering on our commitments is the essential step toward building trust. Over-committing ourselves or our teams often leads to missing targets. The only thing that is achieved is disappointment! While it's important to stretch ourselves and the teams that we lead, we should not do so to the point of getting too far ahead of ourselves. Driving for results means setting stretch targets and then leading the team to achieve them—think, "One foot on the gas, one on the brake."

I recall a time when I was with Unisys. It was during the Y2K timeframe when I took over a large team and a very large government customer program that was losing money to the tune of ~$30M per year. As the leader, I was charged with eliminating those losses. Instead of trying to do it in one fell swoop, I inspired and encouraged the team to look at reducing this loss in increments of $1M at a time by delivering superior results to our customer to re-establish trust and to make good choices that would have long-lasting and impactful results.

I asked the team to help with focusing on smaller achievable increments. This meant we had to achieve a lot of short-term goals to get to our long-term objective, but I didn't want the team to feel like the ultimate goal was unachievable. In this case, I didn't want to outrun the supply wagon; meaning I needed to avoid setting goals in a timeframe that the organization and the company couldn't achieve. In the end, we achieved our goals and even exceeded them for multiple years to come and finished strong with additional contracts and programs being secured and additional customers being added for this same team to support. This incremental, phased approach ensured we could meet our targets while still satisfying the needs of the business and without burning out our team members. I was able to deliver results and thus gain the trust of my organization, the company, and our customers.

Summary

The good news is we don't have to be President Theodore Roosevelt or John Chambers to consistently and reliably demonstrate our Things That Matter. It does, however, require conscious and deliberate effort. With a little planning, a lot of focus, consistent practice, and with the right intent, we can transition Things That Matter from a static list of words to a dynamic lifestyle of authenticity and purpose, which will result in more balanced and confident leadership. This will also lead to inspiring and teaching others to create a repeatable cycle that can become contagious!

> *"Things That Matter is the kind of book every aspiring leader should read early in their journey. Lonnie Essex blends personal stories with practical tools, offering a clear and authentic guide to building leadership that lasts."*
>
> **Arthur Scudeler Brunetti, Retention Manager, Gozney**

Chapter 7: Living Things That Matter

Things That Matter isn't a complex algorithm. You don't need a Ph.D. in psychology to put it into action, and you don't need to be the CEO of a multibillion-dollar corporation. It takes three steps: discover your Things That Matter, communicate them, and demonstrate them. When you sum all that up and deliver it holistically, well, then you're living your Things That Matter. Of course, the true power is in how genuine and authentic you are and how effectively you hold true to the promises you make to others and to yourself. Above all, it's about being open, transparent, and letting others see that. At its core, it's about shaping yourself in order to help others. It's about being a leader of yourself first, then of others.

The "Things That Matter" framework, as presented, is a practical approach to personal and organizational alignment, emphasizing the identification, articulation, and embodiment of core values or beliefs. This framework, while not attributed to a single, universally recognized academic theory in the provided text, aligns with established principles in leadership and personal development. For instance, Stephen Covey's *The 7 Habits of Highly Effective People* emphasizes beginning with the end in mind and putting first things first, which inherently involves identifying what truly matters. Similarly, in organizational contexts, defining and communicating core values is a cornerstone of a strong company culture and strategic alignment, as discussed by experts like Patrick Lencioni in *The Advantage*. The process of "discovering your Things That Matter" can be likened to self-reflection and values clarification exercises common in coaching and personal growth. "Communicate them" directly relates to effective leadership and team building, ensuring shared understanding and purpose. Finally, "demonstrate them" is about living those values through actions, which is crucial for authenticity and building trust, a concept explored in works on ethical leadership and integrity.

Given these references, the cost of admission, therefore, is low. Meaning, anyone anywhere in life, work, partnership, relationships, etc. can benefit from Things That Matter if they earnestly put them into practice. Every day. No cost, no special training, nothing but the talents and skills that life has brought you already.

Any leadership journey can be daunting. It requires us to come to terms with who we are as individuals. For me, this begins with the question: *What are the Things That Matter to me?*

It takes a fair amount of self-awareness to answer that question accurately and honestly. In today's information-saturated world, there is no end to the people and institutions who are happy to tell us what our principles and priorities should be. People with their own agendas who would love nothing more than to co-opt ours. Consider all the things that media—both social and broadcast—throws at us every minute of every day, demanding our attention, our allegiance, and mostly our money. We are constantly being told what to believe and how to act by influencers whose only expertise lies in their ability to get people to click on their content. In this environment, understanding our own minds and our own purposes is almost an act of defiance.

The idea that "understanding our own minds and our own purposes is almost an act of defiance" in this context underscores the challenge of maintaining personal integrity amidst pervasive external influences. In a landscape where algorithms are designed to personalize content feeds and reinforce existing biases, actively seeking out diverse perspectives and engaging in self-reflection becomes crucial for developing a robust sense of self and purpose.

Now, clearly, people have had Things That Matter to them a long time before I came along. Having principles, values, and beliefs is nothing new. It's not even difficult. In fact, it's downright intuitive. Now, framing them up, documenting them, communicating them, and then demonstrating them is a whole other thing. Very few people ever do this.

As we identify and define our Things That Matter, we need to remember to pause and to breathe. Answering the question, "What are the Things That Matter to me?" takes patience and deliberation. Don't be distressed if you struggle to pin down your thoughts, if you find you change your mind, if it takes longer than you had assumed. You are essentially answering the questions:

1. Who are you?
2. What are you about?
3. What are you made of?
4. What makes you, you?
5. What is my purpose?

These are big questions that humankind has struggled with since the beginning of time. The trick is not to be overwhelmed by them. My suggestion: break it down into chunks. Be systematic. Relax. Make a list of three or four Things That Matter to you, let them percolate, then add some more. Take time to define them, test them, reflect on them. Are they authentic? Do you naturally align with them in your thinking and your behaviors? Can you live them?

There is a children's book written by Laura Joffe Numeroff and illustrated by Felicia Bond called *If You Give a Mouse a Cookie*. The premise is captured in the very first line. "If you give a mouse a cookie, he's going to ask for a glass of milk." The point is one thing naturally leads to another. A bit of cause and effect. What naturally follows from identifying your Things That Matter is communicating them to others.

"If you identify your Things That Matter, you're going to need to tell people about them."

As you develop your Things That Matter, it makes sense to get validation from those closest to you. In the end, you own these and must communicate and demonstrate them, but a small amount of validation during the development process may help you narrow your list or ideally just confirm what you were already thinking. For example, if one of your Things That Matter is going to be "Helping Others," your closest friends and allies can validate if this is something that readily aligns with you or if it is something that should be aspirational for you. Meaning you may want to get there, but in fact you are not there yet.

Talk about your Things That Matter. Socialize them. Every time we talk about our Things That Matter to others, we recommit ourselves to living them. In this way, sharing them actually helps to keep us honest. Say them out loud and you are instantly committed. It is like re-recording voice mail we discussed earlier…The second or third versions net much better than the very first one! For instance, I encourage my teams and colleagues to tell me if they see me doing things that run counter to my Things That Matter. To call me out if you will. And here's the thing: even if they never do, the idea that they *might* sticks with me. Without telling others, it would only be me holding myself accountable. If I got off track, no one would be the wiser. **With no accountability, there is little incentive to ever stay on course.** It begs the rhetorical question if no one was present to hear or provide comments, would you still believe what you are expressing or were you telling people what they wanted to hear? This is how people get lost. Leadership can be a wilderness. Accountability, both to oneself and to others, serves as a crucial mechanism for maintaining one's moral and ethical direction, often referred to as an "internal compass" or "true north." Self-accountability involves taking responsibility for one's own actions, decisions, and their consequences. It is an internal commitment to uphold personal values, goals, and standards, regardless of external pressures or oversight. This internal drive fosters self-discipline and integrity, enabling individuals to align their behavior with their TTM.

Along these lines, a powerful signal to others is to actually call yourself out if you've noticed you have contradicted one of your Things That Matter. In these situations, chances are that others have noticed too, but they're just too polite to confront you. It can be a cathartic moment to admit to yourself and others when you've strayed from one of your principles. It tells them you're not infallible and that you're trying to do better.

So, once you've identified your Things That Matter—a process that takes considerable self-honesty and reflection—and once you have communicated them to others and thus have created a contract of accountability—a process that takes bravery and commitment; as a reminder, the next step is to actually do something with them—to "get action."

Now, as we think about getting action, we think about making things happen, about being a driver of change, we tend to place ourselves as the doer of that action. It's a natural impulse. We place ourselves as the heroes of our own stories. Again, there's nothing wrong with this. In fact, I would suggest it's healthy. It places us in the focus of control. Every leader needs to be accountable, every leader needs to be a driver, to have the capacity to make things happen, to make the news or change the news and not just report it. This is a good and healthy place to find oneself, but at the same time, there comes a point in everyone's leadership journey when they need to shift from thinking about themselves to thinking about their teams.

In most people's careers, there is a period when they believe they can do it all on their own. Many people fall into the trap of believing that not only can they do it all by themselves, but that if it's going to get done right, then they have to do it themselves. These are the micromanagers, the people who re-do everyone's work, the people who can't let go, who are unable to delegate. **It's easy at first to command and control...until it isn't.** People who fall into this trap usually burn out early in their careers and create a lot of enemies and hard feelings along the way.

For some, this period of hyper-control is a necessary step in their journey. Again, we learn from our mistakes. I've known many micromanagers who grew out of that phase and into fantastic leaders. It may have been an unpleasant path for them and those around them, but they learned the hard way!

People who are able to pull themselves out of this trap usually do so by realizing that they can't grow or expand by doing everything solo. It simply takes too much time and energy. It also prevents them from taking on bigger, more strategic matters. They soon discover they can't solve every problem, and there just aren't enough hours in a day or days in a week to get it all done. When you make 100% of the decisions and the team fails, who is to blame—you! Those who progress past this point are those who realize others around them can help. They recognize that if they can build a great team, a culture, then that team probably can solve most if not all the challenges.

Visualize this, I think of leadership in terms of helping team members to get many wheels spinning in the same direction, then having the same individuals directly responsible for each individual wheel, while the leader continues to check in with each team member to ensure that each wheel maintains a consistent and constant forward momentum and direction. When I was a child, we would turn our bicycles upside down and spin the front wheel as a contest to see which wheel would spin for the longest time. Once the wheel was spinning, you could only apply a light touch of energy to keep it spinning, which in reality was all that it needed. If you tried to step in and apply too much energy, it would actually cause the wheel to turn slower and therefore prevent consistent and constant momentum. As a leader, this will primarily be your task every day to Measure and Monitor (inspect) progress and ensure that your team has all of their wheels turning efficiently and to help them remove barriers and be successful (remember One Foot on the Gas and One on the Brake).

For me, this inflection point came when I moved from a small networking company to Unisys, which at the time still topped seven billion in annual revenue per year. The P&L for my organization was enormous, the largest in my career. I was excited about the challenge. The sector was rapidly growing, and it felt like we were at the forefront of it. I was also humble and a bit nervous.

That type of responsibility comes with a fair amount of risk. Certainly, a lot could go right, but a lot could also go wrong. There was a lot at stake, and I would be carrying the burden. For one panic-filled moment, I could feel the massive weight bearing down upon my shoulders. To be honest, I wasn't sure I was up for the task…and then it dawned on me. I didn't have to do it alone. In fact, I probably *couldn't* do it alone. At least not for long. And so, I had a choice to make.

As I saw it, there was one option where I could charge in and try to do everything. I could exert full control, work fourteen hours a day every weekday and every weekend, even vacations. I could fully dedicate myself to my work and, as a byproduct, ignore my other obligations, forget my family and friends, and drive myself to an early grave. A blaze of glory, bright but short-lived. Option one wasn't pretty, though I knew more than one person who took that path.

Thankfully, there was a second option. Option two involved distributing that burden over a larger surface area. Metal sinks in water, but a well-crafted metal hull can not only float but can also carry a substantial cargo.

What if I built a strong team around me with the diversity, expertise and professionalism needed to get the job done? A team I could delegate to, a team that could be trusted to deliver. What if I built a team centered on a common set of values? In this scenario, I could see that team taking on the challenges I knew would come with that massive P&L. I envisioned such a team not only meeting the required obligations but expanding past that remit and actually growing the business.

What I realized was this: **getting the right people (Trusted Resources) into the right roles with clear responsibilities along**

with targeted training and documented processes is one of the most impactful and important things you will do as a leader. Do this well, and your teams will likely succeed. Otherwise, your teams will be confused, frustrated, disappointed, exhausted…and after all of that, they will probably face failure on many levels. This will impact your customers and partners as well, so take care NOT to let this happen.

As soon as I understood it wasn't about me, my fear subsided. It was about my team and the organization. If done right, there was nothing but upside. I was surrounded by many Trusted Resources—individuals who were bright and energetic and who wanted to contribute, who were experts and leaders in their own specialties with years of experience. They needed me to lead the charge, but they were ready and willing to lead their parts for the team.

It also dawned on me that in this scenario the entire team would benefit and not just me. The entire team would have a chance to improve their capabilities and their salaries and bonuses. And as they grew, the company would grow. That seemed like a much better outcome than just one person benefiting.

Things That Matter begin with one person, but if it never extends past that one person, it serves zero purpose. Things That Matter is best leveraged through others and for others. Things That Matter should reside as a list on your phone (or sticky note on your computer) where they serve as a ready reminder and resource; they then should surface in conversations you have with your team and colleagues and serve as a point of accountability; and they most certainly should be demonstrated in your actions throughout the day, the week, the month. They should exist in all these places, but you will know you have succeeded when your Things That Matter take root in the culture of your team, your organization, your circle of influence and among your Trusted Resources. That's when you will know you are truly living your Things That Matter.

Seven Levels of Done

Ownership (TTM #3) is a Core attribute in my Things That Matter. It is a value that I believe is important for me to live out personally. I also believe Ownership is important for teams and the companies or organizations they support. Now, I can go around all day talking about the importance of ownership. I can strive to demonstrate it in my actions. I can even reward team members who exhibit ownership of their own behavior. I can also take it a step further and seek to instill different aspects of Ownership into the way my team operates. I can in a sense weave it into the fabric of our culture. An example of this is something I call "Seven Levels of Done."

Throughout my entire work history, whether in sales or operations, whether I was reporting up or others were reporting to me, or usually both, I have noticed a phenomenon that has replicated itself in any organization I have ever worked. Whether it was the grocery stores in my youth, the military in my early career, or any of the technology firms in my later career, people always tended to report something as being "done" long before it was actually 100% complete. I'm not saying people lied. I'm not saying they intentionally claimed something was finalized when they in fact knew that it wasn't. In every instance, the people involved honestly felt the task or process was indeed done…but it wasn't. How can this be? How could they have sincerely thought something was completed when in fact it was not?

After seeing this happen countless times firsthand, I came to realize that there's a communication gap that often occurs, especially as it relates to selling and delivering complex integrated projects. I recall a time years ago when my team was working on a large installation for an important customer. Granted, in my book all customers are important, but we'll just say this one represented a sizable opportunity. In other words, not someone we wanted to disappoint.

After working on the project for several weeks, with the customer anxious for us to be done and us anxious to deliver excellent service, my project manager informed the customer's project manager we were done working at their location. That comment rapidly escalated up their chain of command, fueled by the fact that nothing was actually working at the site. Emails were sent; phone calls were made. The customer was not only disappointed but angry. Their top management informed our top management, and things rapidly worked through our organization until my phone rang. *Houston, we have a problem.*

It didn't take long to get to the bottom of the situation. When I spoke to the project manager, he said, "I think I misspoke. I said we were done, but we weren't done-done."

What he meant to convey to the customer was, "We have completed the physical installation stage of the project. The team responsible for that work is done. We will now be moving on to the next stage of the project."

But of course, that's not what the customer heard.

The project manager's comment of "we're done" only pertained to physically running cables and connecting devices. The "we" in his "we're done" meant the crew responsible for those duties. There was still programming, configuration, user acceptance testing, training, and more to be done. This can easily apply to residential and commercial construction as well, where there are many trades delivering tasks and features that may be declared "done," but until all tasks and features are done, the overall project is NOT "done-done!"

I wondered, can there really be two levels of done or is it really more? I thought about it. I took notes, I conferred with others, I sifted through my own experiences. I concluded that there were not two levels of done; there were, in fact, Seven Levels of Done!

It's one of those things that's only funny after you get some distance from it. I recall so many instances of quizzing team members and asking, "What do you mean it's done? Where is it? Is the order received? Have the funds cleared? Has the product been delivered?" It seemed that every person had a different idea of what "done" meant. What I found was that it mostly pertained to one small aspect they were in charge of as opposed to the much larger process the company was delivering. This might be slightly annoying with a small order, but when it's a ten-million-dollar deal, it's a whole other story. **As a leader,**

you must always ensure that your team takes ownership of outcomes and results until they are 100% done-done! If you think you are done-done and the customer or partner doesn't agree, then a final payment is typically withheld, which creates lots of issues that require all parties to sort out which leads to an undesirable customer experience.

This particular issue was especially vexing to me because it ran counter to how I thought about Ownership. Ownership, after all, was number three of my Things That Matter, and yet some members of my own organization still weren't getting it. I wondered how I could emphasize Ownership in such a way that it would get into the culture of my team and allied teams. We all needed to speak the same language around the simple concept of "done." And so, I developed a framework I call Seven Levels of Done, and now I share it with all my teams. Over the years I've refined it to specific types of work I'm mostly involved in, such as pre- and post-sales. In post-sales, the seven levels include a "System Done" level, which involves system initialization and verification. Here, we focus on operational readiness. The system is powered up, all components function as expected, and the software operates with the installed hardware. This is much different from a later level of done called "Enterprise Resource Planning (ERP) Done." In this stage, the 'project completed' option is selected in the ERP system, signifying the formal closure of the project. All documentation, including final billings, trailing costs, and any other project paperwork, is completed and submitted. As final as "ERP Done" seems, it is only level six. The last level of done in all the "Seven Levels of Done" I have ever developed is, of course, "Done-Done."

Today when one of my team members tells me, "We're done with the project," I respond with "Which level of done?" When they respond, "Level Seven—we're done-done," well, it's time to celebrate. Which we do. A job well done is a job worth celebrating. If you want to learn more about my "Seven Levels of Done" Framework, please visit my website at Lonnieessex.com

You can apply the "Seven Levels of Done" Framework to any industry, sales engagement, project, or task as a means to Effectively Communicate to all stakeholders up, down, or sideways whether something is really 100% done! The beauty of the framework is in its portability. That is, it can spread throughout organizations. When one person sees that it works for them, they adopt it and use it with other people they work with. In this way, Ownership goes beyond being a personal agenda item for me as one person and takes root in the company's culture. This is the power of Things That Matter.

Things That Matter is more than a list and more than a single person demonstrating certain behaviors. As we develop and implement our Things That Matter, we should look for opportunities to embed them in our sphere of influence, whether that's a family, a team that you lead, or an entire organization or company.

Influence vs. Control

If we want our teams, our organizations, and those around us to be successful, then we have to have standards to build our culture upon. As leaders, those standards begin with us. They begin with answering the question, "What are the Things That Matter to me?" Once we answer that question, we need to communicate it, and then we're going to need to demonstrate those standards—to be serious about them, to stick to them, to live them. To do this, we will need to embed these standards not only in our daily actions, but in our processes and ways of working.

But what about situations in which we don't lead a team? How do we inspire others to drive change, achieve common goals, deliver positive outcomes, or solve major challenges when those others don't actually report to us?

I often work with individuals who are emerging as sales or operations leaders. I coach them, mentor them, sponsor them. One insight I always share is the fact that as they rise into higher levels of leadership, they'll have less direct control over driving change, strategy, or policy. A lot of people are surprised by this. Standard wisdom dictates that the higher one goes in an organization, the more control they have. The reality is that most businesses operate through delegations of authority. Through this design, one person is accountable for the ultimate outcomes and results, while the responsibility to take action to deliver those outcomes and results is delegated to others. One's ability to be successful, therefore, increasingly depends on one's ability to influence others.

When I work with emerging leaders, I encourage them to take on a methodical approach when leading initiatives and guiding teams. There are four key considerations I recommend: Control, Influence, Work Around (with caution), and, when all else fails, Move On.

Control

First, there is the question of control. As discussed, early in our careers, we may feel more in control because we can just do things ourselves. Typically, in one's early career, they start in a tactical role focusing on process-oriented tasks. These roles are essential to any workforce. The joy at this level of work is the hands-on aspect of it. The opportunity to get our "hands dirty," whether it's with a physical tool or with a spreadsheet, can be gratifying. But that doesn't scale—and it's not true leadership.

As we elevate through the ranks, we will begin taking on the role of managing others who do that work. As our responsibilities grow and we lead teams (or even lead leaders of teams), we'll have to let go of control. What's more, as we rise in an organization, we will have to rely on people who likely in no way, shape, or form, report to us. This is commonly called using Influence Management. They may report to entirely different divisions or business lines, and we will need to rely on our ability to influence them rather than control. That can be uncomfortable, especially if you're used to being hands-on, but leadership is about influencing others to take ownership and execute collectively.

Influence

For some people, the idea of losing direct control is frightening. The same people are also often frightened by the prospect of having to influence others to get results. There is nothing wrong with this reaction. Ask any parent who has tried to teach a teenager to drive. It's much easier to drive a car safely than it is to influence someone to drive a car safely. The reality, though, is that in today's workplace, change happens through collaboration, teamwork, and influence. This is especially true as we progress through the ranks of management and leadership. Modern agile leaders need to master these skills to drive initiatives and achieve outcomes. This means building alliances across departments and securing sponsorship from other leaders.

I recommend a "big tent" approach instead of the divisive approach used so often today. Modern agile leaders need to effectively manage up, down, and across levels, teams, organizations, and stakeholders to stay close enough to what is or isn't happening but also not too close *(remember the spinning bicycle wheels)*. They must be able to navigate political waters and know when to push and when to yield. You can't effectively lead by sitting behind a desk or on back-to-back virtual calls all day staring at dashboards and spreadsheets. Those things are essential but not enough. You must be agile, and you must listen to the words, the mood, the sentiment, the body language. You must be present!

A "big tent" approach in business is a strategy where a company seeks to unite diverse stakeholders under a common goal, emphasizing that supporting the company's objectives ultimately benefits everyone involved. This strategy is particularly effective in complex environments where various groups might have differing immediate interests but share a long-term dependency on the company's success. It involves fostering a sense of shared purpose and demonstrating how individual contributions, no matter how varied, contribute to a larger, mutually beneficial outcome.

When using a 'big tent' approach, we appeal to the idea that it's in everyone's best interest to support the company's goals. That may mean stepping out of our comfort zone to help a colleague work through a problem they're struggling with. It may mean taking on extra work that may not be part of our remit. But as soon as we realize that we're all in this together, that if our colleague fails, we also fail because the organization's ability to achieve its goal is weakened, then the complaint of "not my problem" starts to fade.

When we help others in our organization, they're more likely to help us. By building a network of virtuous support, the whole enterprise benefits. It's amazing to me that so many people talk about inclusiveness, but when it comes time to actually exercise it, they balk at the prospect. Unity toward a common goal, supported at the right levels and enacted inclusively, is at the heart of influence. **When you can't Control, you must Influence**.

In the past year in my current full-time leadership role, I've been able to lead a team to achieve success with a new multi-year training roadmap for our division and the subsequent first course that has been taken by hundreds of employees. This required significant collaboration, input, modeling, content shaping, prioritization, influence, and negotiation. Originally, the goal was to launch many more courses along this multi-year roadmap in the first year, but the team decided on fewer courses that have higher quality and greater impact.

To achieve that goal, we had to influence dozens of stakeholders and work around dozens of obstacles while staying within the usual budget and resource limitations and other competing priorities. In the end, we gained alignment on a way forward that would deliver the desired results. Gaining that alignment took more time and certainly more finesse than it would have if we had owned the entire process end-to-end and if we had had complete control over the rest of the company. In truth, that type of command and control rarely exists in any modern organization with the possible exception of the military. **The ability to influence is a major required skill in the leadership toolkit.**

Work Around (With Caution)

At times, there will be situations when our influence is not enough. Again, think Predictive Follow-up (TTM #6). Perhaps there is not enough time, or we just can't get enough critical mass to secure the right amount of support or sponsorship. In these cases, we might be tempted to work around barriers. Sometimes this is necessary but be cautious. Organizational culture, politics, and internal alliances can make this risky. Understand the environment before taking this route. Meaning, trying to drive initiatives forward may feel rewarding and productive in the moment, but if it causes stress or damage elsewhere in the organization, then you must decide if it is really worth it politically and culturally. Command and Control type leaders are more likely to pursue this approach at any cost, versus how a more Collaborative and Agile leader may know to avoid this maneuver.

As an example, earlier this year, I held a roundtable with my team centered on a Stop, Start, Continue exercise. As previously noted, this is a great method to get input from everyone, to practice Listening (TTM #2), and to Acknowledge Contributions (TTM #5). It has many benefits and often solves organizational challenges through an Employee First approach (TTM #6). At the same time, this exercise almost always leads to Continuous Improvement (TTM #9).

This particular session resulted in an avalanche of ideas. They were all excellent ideas, which would have solved a great number of our challenges and enhanced several areas of our operations. The reality, though, was that with limited budgets, resources, and time. Many of the ideas would have required collaboration, buy-in, and support from other stakeholders.

Rather than saying "no" to everything, I brought this complication for the team to consider. Very quickly, they were able to consolidate themes and organize the feedback into a few categories. We then gained agreement and ratified the inputs, prioritized the top initiatives and assigned owners within the context of very real constraints such as budget, resources, and time. In this instance, the team consolidated what would have been multiple efforts into streamlined initiatives that would deliver the same results.

In addition, the team was able to assess what they had direct control over and what would require influence and alignment with other organizations. The residual were activities and initiatives that needed to be Worked Around to avoid the team taking on work that would yield very little or no results due to existing constraints and the balance of priorities. The team was able to then make a call on what they could reasonably achieve and what they would leave on the table, for now. The realization was that if they took on too much, they would fail. Failure would lead to disappointment and low morale on the team, not to mention a drop in the company's confidence in the team to deliver on commitments, which would have its own cascade of negative effects.

Work Around (with caution) is sometimes the best route to take when there are too many competing priorities or if resources are limited. They are not always easy decisions to make and require strong leadership resolve to ensure that everyone has input and an ability to be heard, while balancing what is possible to achieve, gaining consensus around those things and then proceeding to get things done given macro and micro impediments. Work Around may simply mean "not now." It could be a great idea that needs to be prioritized. When the timing isn't right to proceed to get budget, resources, or support from others, waiting for the right time to push forward is a form of Work Around. Negotiating with other stakeholders or teams or outsourcing tasks can also be a Work Around.

Move On

And finally, there will be times when, despite our best efforts, we can't Control, Influence, or even Work Around situations. Good leaders know when it's time to move on. They focus on where their teams can make an impact. In these scenarios, we have to ask ourselves and our teams: *How can we move forward and accomplish our other important goals?*

This often equates to saying "no" to some initiatives, project requests, or priorities. Good leaders must know when and where to invest time and Trusted Resources in initiatives or projects that may actually be achievable. At times, you may say "no" initially based on the challenges your team faces. And other times, you may proceed only to find the team is unable to influence or work around challenges in an effective or timely manner. In these cases, the leader must be able to look at the landscape and avoid having the team expend valuable resources, only to subsequently fail the objective. Leaders must continually inspect and re-assess all initiatives and projects to potentially shift resources or know when to say stop.

While at Cisco, one year at the Annual Cisco Directors' Conference, John Chambers announced bold steps to launch thirty-plus strategic initiatives which, at the time, seemed futile. He felt like setting a lofty goal would motivate the various teams to go for it on each and every one of them. I felt like this was definitely a case of Outrunning the Supply Wagon, but as a good Cisco leader, I fell in line behind all the initiatives, some of which were not related to my area of leadership. Soon after, Chambers realized this was far too many strategic initiatives and had to cut down. Everyone knew that the company was serious about growth, driving change, and achieving remarkable results. In this case, Chambers had to re-assess the total number and decide to prioritize our focus on several large, strategic and impactful initiatives and then move on.

Modern agile leaders know when to say "no," when to re-assess the battlefield, and when to make new decisions for their teams in order to achieve as much success as possible in as many areas as possible.

A compelling business example illustrating modern agile leaders' ability to say "no," re-assess the battlefield, and make new decisions for their teams to achieve widespread success can be found in the evolution of Netflix's content strategy. Initially, Netflix was primarily a DVD-by-mail rental service. As technology advanced and streaming became viable, their leaders recognized the shift in the "battlefield" of entertainment consumption. They made the bold decision to say "no" to solely relying on their highly successful DVD business model and instead invested heavily in streaming technology and content licensing.

What Matters to You?

Whether we are individual contributors, whether we have direct teams we manage, or a network we influence, what matters to us as individuals can have a positive effect on those around us. I believe that we all have talents, and we all have strengths. We all also have shortcomings and weaknesses. Each of us has a unique profile of attributes that makes us, us. We shouldn't strive to maximize all of our attributes. It simply isn't possible. There is no one perfect person. In fact, I would argue that it's the combination of our strengths and weaknesses that makes us interesting. It's nature's fail-safe to make sure we cooperate with one another.

When I mentor others, I start with, "You're good at something, right? You may not be good at everything that you want to excel at, but you've got to practice and apply yourself. It starts with finding out what you're good at. What you enjoy doing. Do that. Do more of that."

Most people don't believe that what matters to them can make a difference to those around them, so they keep it to themselves. The truth is everyone has value; everyone wants to and can contribute. It doesn't always seem that way, but what matters to you can make a difference to those around you. But it won't happen by accident. You have to be the driver; you have to get action.

I learned a very long time ago that the world and the circumstances within it are not always kind. In fact, they can be downright cruel. I lost both of my parents by age twelve. Luckily, the time I had with them was filled with valuable lessons that I could carry with me and build upon. Those lessons weren't packaged with bows and ribbons— life is not always kind nor fair—but throughout those years and throughout my career I took time to notice, to heed, to learn. I followed my internal compass, which indicated that there were indeed things in life, in the world, in the workplace, that matter more than others.

These became my Things That Matter. I'm not suggesting they should be your Things That Matter, though some might. You should discover your own Things That Matter. They should come from your life, from your experiences.

So, I ask: what matters to you?

Reflect on them, document them, communicate them, demonstrate them, live them, embed them. Adjust them when needed. Be flexible but always be authentic. The results will be success and confidence not only for you as an individual but for your teams, your family, and those around you who become part of your journey.

"What makes this book special is how it blends story with strategy. You'll find real experiences, memorable lessons, and concrete steps for uncovering your own Things That Matter and weaving them into every aspect of your career and life. Whether you're an aspiring leader, a seasoned executive, or simply someone who wants to live with more intention, Things That Matter is the kind of book you'll return to again and again to enjoy the heart and wisdom behind each page."

Patricia Gonzalez, CEO, Real Talk Coaching and Consulting Services

Epilogue: Coming Home

Leadership is about helping others, inspiring, encouraging, and motivating them to achieve common goals. I compare it to a sports team, maybe a community social activity. It really applies to all aspects of life.

Leadership, in its essence, is a multifaceted discipline centered on guiding individuals or groups toward the accomplishment of shared objectives. It transcends mere authority, encompassing a blend of interpersonal skills, strategic foresight, and a commitment to fostering growth and collaboration. The analogy to a sports team or a community social activity is apt, as effective leadership in these contexts, much like in professional settings, relies on the ability to unite diverse talents, inspire collective effort, and navigate challenges together.

At its core, leadership involves several key components. **One primary aspect is the establishment of a clear vision and direction.** A leader articulates where the team or organization is headed, providing a roadmap that aligns individual efforts with overarching goals. This vision acts as a unifying force, giving purpose and meaning to the work being done. Another crucial element is the capacity to inspire and motivate. This goes beyond simply giving orders; it involves understanding the needs and aspirations of team members, fostering a positive and supportive environment, and recognizing contributions. Motivation can be intrinsic, stemming from a sense of purpose and achievement, or extrinsic, through recognition and rewards.

Not long ago, I had the opportunity to orchestrate a memorial tribute for my father's hundredth birthdate. It was a big project with invitations, an overarching theme, a program of events, catering, and decorations—the works. To capture the event for future generations, we had a photographer and a videographer. I also enlisted the help of my siblings and other family members. You could say that I led it, but I didn't do it all myself. I even got the local American Legion Post 107, Soddy-Daisy, TN to participate. They came and formally started the tribute with the Posting of Colors and even dedicated a few words for my father's service. I set the stage, I painted a picture of what we wanted to achieve, and I got a lot of other people excited and motivated to contribute, and they did. In this case, it became more of a civic function than a family function.

It was October 2024, so it was a bit chilly. It was in my hometown in Tennessee—Soddy-Daisy. The setting was a community center associated with a church that my family has been a part of for a long time. I had taken photos of my father throughout his life, and I had poster-size blowups made—my father as a young man in the military, midlife, later in life—and I put them on easels as a backdrop. Then we had a lectern and mic and all. My stepson, Jose, led the group in the National Anthem, which was very touching, as you can imagine. My siblings and I all got up and said a few words, and I asked them each to come up with a memory or a story that changed or touched their lives. The American Legion re-dedicated my father's funeral flag, originally presented to our family fifty years ago. Presented to my eldest sister.

People took selfies and group photos next to the large photographs. You could hear people saying over and over in a variety of ways, "Oh, I remember that. I know that picture so well."

There were about sixty people in attendance. Family, friends, and we had a live band so people could sing or do karaoke. Then, of course, food and all. My brother and I have birthdays two days apart in

October, so we had a giant cake for my brother, me, and my father. It would've been his hundredth birthday in August 2024.

All in all, it was a touching event. I was pleased with the outcome. I was pleased because so many people loved it, found joy in it. The result of a lot of effort by a lot of people. They say that in cooking it's all about the ingredients. As I planned and coordinated the event, I could see all of my ten Things That Matter—the ingredients, if you will—come into play.

It was almost all about Effective Communication; there was Ownership, Seeking Assistance, Acknowledging Contributions, even Curiosity. I could make an exhaustive list and provide proof points, but the fact that all my Things That Matter were in action isn't the real point. The real point is they worked together to have an impact on others. We celebrated a patriotic and benevolent life, and we recognized the positive impact that life had on us.

Not far from where we held the tribute is the land where we grew up and our grocery store was. It's no longer there; time has marched on. Now there are houses. Those houses are filled with the families of my siblings, and those families are making their own memories and carving out their own paths.

It occurs to me that no matter how far I go in life and in my career, I never stray too far from home. Geographically I may not live in Soddy-Daisy, but the things I learned there, the people that started me on my way…well, we share that common root. And for that, I will always be grateful.

This book was written to appeal to a multi-generational audience, so I hope new and emerging leaders, or even experienced leaders that need a reset, have gained valuable insights about themselves. Most importantly, you must "walk the talk." If you get off track, you can always come back to your curated and documented list.

Discovering what is important in my life, my Things That Matter, has been a journey. Those values, the principles that make up my Things That Matter, are a bit of home that I carry with me wherever I go. I wish you all the best on your journey, and I hope you may find and hold true to your Things That Matter and pass it on to others.

Lonnie's Favorite Sayings

These are a few phrases (mostly in the book) that I find myself coming back to, which reinforce many of my TTM and hopefully inspire others:

- "Get Action"
- "That's how you run the railroad"
- "Too busy chopping wood to sharpen your ax"
- "One on the gas and one on the brake"
- "By design, not by default"
- "Don't outrun the supply wagon"
- "Be inspirational, not didactic"
- "Catch people doing the right things"
- "Be consistent and persistent"
- "Don't suffer in silence"

I look forward to bringing you more adventures in the future!

Acknowledgement

Life is made more enjoyable and meaningful by the company you keep along the way. I would like to thank the many people who have helped me along on my own journey.

I would first like to thank my wife, Pamela Alcantara Essex, who has always believed in me and who has always demonstrated unwavering support. Pamela is my closest advisor and has made me a better person.

I would also like to thank my parents and my siblings, who provided the lessons and experiences that would be the genesis of my Things That Matter. My father, George Essex, was a leader in the community and a leader in our family as well as among our extended family. My eldest sister, Norma, who became my legal guardian and the family leader after my mother, Mary Catherine, and then my father, George, passed away at an early age.

There were also so many leaders, mentors, friends, and colleagues who inspired me and helped me to learn and grow. While there are too many to list everyone here, I would especially like to acknowledge these individuals who had a major impact on me and to whom I am forever grateful.

- Colonel Alfred R. Garcia, Jr., USAF
- Gary Lau: White House Communications Agency and N.E.T. Federal
- Tom Semmes: White House Communications Agency
- Bob Krueger: N.E.T. Federal

- Thomas J (TJ) Miller: N.E.T. Federal and Unisys
- Jenafer (Bell) Howard: N.E.T. Federal and Cisco
- Gene Buckley: Cisco Systems
- George O'Meara: Cisco Systems
- Katie Valle: AVI-SPL

Book Content Coaches and Advisors: A very special thanks to those that helped me write and shape this book.
- Kate Peters: Writer, Production Management, Content Management, Advisor.
- Gary Hernandez: Making my words, thoughts, and notes come to life with amazing writing.
- George O'Meara: Former Cisco executive and manager, author, friend, and advisor. George provided additional value in each and every chapter and made the end product more impactful!

Launch Advisors: Writing a book is a lot of work, and then launching a book is equally challenging. This team got me through all the steps and details required for a successful launch.
- Pamela Alcantara Essex
- Kelly Dias
- Fady Ramzy
- Arthur Brunetti
- Camilla Fano – Cover Concept
- Maryssa Gordon, Pocket Editing
- Marisela Dominguez – Graphic Design

By now you know that my favorite quote is "Get Action" by President Teddy Roosevelt. I apply this approach in all parts of life to ensure forward progress. I hope this book has made you a better leader and a better person in general, who positively impacts your enterprise and those around you.

Thank you for reading!

www.ingramcontent.com/pod-product-compliance
Lightning Source LLC
Chambersburg PA
CBHW030221170426
43194CB00007BA/815